Collective Forgiveness

Oliver Errichiello

Collective Forgiveness

The Constructive Power of an Enigmatic Feeling

Oliver Errichiello
Büro für Markenentwicklung
Hamburg, Hamburg, Germany

This book is a translation of the original German edition „Kollektives Verzeihen" by Errichiello, Oliver, published by Springer-Verlag GmbH, DE in 2021. The translation was done with the help of artificial intelligence (machine translation by the service DeepL.com). A subsequent human revision was done primarily in terms of content, so that the book will read stylistically differently from a conventional translation. Springer Nature works continuously to further the development of tools for the production of books and on the related technologies to support the authors.

ISBN 978-3-662-63910-8   ISBN 978-3-662-63911-5 (eBook)
https://doi.org/10.1007/978-3-662-63911-5

© Springer-Verlag GmbH Germany, part of Springer Nature 2021
This work is subject to copyright. All rights are reserved by the Publisher, whether the whole or part of the material is concerned, specifically the rights of translation, reprinting, reuse of illustrations, recitation, broadcasting, reproduction on microfilms or in any other physical way, and transmission or information storage and retrieval, electronic adaptation, computer software, or by similar or dissimilar methodology now known or hereafter developed.
The use of general descriptive names, registered names, trademarks, service marks, etc. in this publication does not imply, even in the absence of a specific statement, that such names are exempt from the relevant protective laws and regulations and therefore free for general use.
The publisher, the authors, and the editors are safe to assume that the advice and information in this book are believed to be true and accurate at the date of publication. Neither the publisher nor the authors or the editors give a warranty, expressed or implied, with respect to the material contained herein or for any errors or omissions that may have been made. The publisher remains neutral with regard to jurisdictional claims in published maps and institutional affiliations.

This Springer imprint is published by the registered company Springer-Verlag GmbH, DE part of Springer Nature.
The registered company address is: Heidelberger Platz 3, 14197 Berlin, Germany

For Morten and Bent

Foreword: "Forgiveness—The Limits of Rationality"

People with convictions are to be envied. From the infinite confusion of knowledge, information, and opinions, they sharpen their picture of the world. Their views become messages. Messages convey more than just information because they want to "share" knowledge. Mostly by referencing on existing things, i.e., views, experiences, to strengthen or secure the bond with others. Messages create groups of like-minded people due to their anchoring and exclude others precisely because of this, who in turn form groups themselves. Opinions are so important because they multiply, order, stabilize, and—in their corridor—constantly renew convictions. In times of supposed individualism, a difficult thought. In the epoch of postmodern addiction to harmony, opinions are an announcement of disruption.

Beliefs and messages are the fuel of coexistence. In their general access and as the object of group formation, they create islands of ideas, significances that struggle to assert themselves. Sometimes to the point of "living apart" or arguing. For opinions are characterized by being deeply "prejudice-laden." Opinions do not pretend to be inclusive.

They integrate points of view that underscore their own beliefs. Opinions are free—that is their very characteristic. Their justification lies in themselves.

One's conviction or the conviction of a group is something deeply human and illustrates both the hubris, the self-overestimation but also the own limitation of every human being. For even on the basis of identical facts, we may come to different judgments. The modern world, with its economic, social, and environmental challenges, produces an infinite level of complexity that makes it impossible to fully assess any given set of facts. This sometimes results in incomprehension and disagreement. However, living together needs dissent, needs the constructive-tolerant lack of understanding of the other—knowing that one's point of view is also just a point of view. And it is precisely at this point that "forgiveness" comes into play.

Against the backdrop of a zeitgeist that tries to quantify and measure everything, forgiveness represents one of the last bastions of irrationality. We forgive, although mostly all reasons speak against it. This is what distinguishes the strange human from a logical algorithm. And yet, when examined closely, the dynamics are profoundly rational and forward-looking.

This book is an invitation to every reader to become more aware of obvious and hidden actions—and to recognize that it is not only we as individuals who act in communities but also the community within us.

Contents

1. What Does Collective Forgiveness Mean? 1
2. About Favor and Autonomy 17
3. About Forgiveness 35
4. About the Collective Will 47
5. About Opinions of Many 61
6. About the Collective Forgiveness 77
7. Final Thoughts on: Why Forgiveness Makes us Human 83

About the Author

 **Oliver Errichiello** studied socioeconomics and analytical psychology at the University of Hamburg and the University of Lyon. In 2006, he founded the Büro für Markenentwicklung. Oliver Errichiello is a lecturer for brand sociology and advertising and consumer psychology at the University of Applied Studies in Lucerne and Bremen. In 2018, the University of Applied Studies Mittweida appointed him honorary professor. He is co-organizer of the lecture series "Community and Society" and "Morality and Ethics" at the University of Hamburg.

1

What Does Collective Forgiveness Mean?

There is hardly any experience that moves us as much as forgiving. Forgiveness has been around ever since people have been willingly coming into contact with people, thinking about the future, and their hopes, expectations, perhaps even dreams have not been fulfilled in the way they thought, wished or hoped for. Perhaps because the other person has consciously or unconsciously acted differently than expected. We withdraw disappointed, break off contact if possible—for good or for a certain time. Something in us urges reflection, relieves the feeling of dejection, disillusionment, even anger - sometimes. Hurts linger or fade away. Everyone has had to experience disappointment in another - regardless of whether that subjective assessment is justified. And probably every person has been forgiven and probably every one of us has said, "It's okay," or at important moments, "I forgive you." Forgiveness is based on trust. We forgive because we trust that the other person will again act as we expect, as has been the custom in the relationship. Trust is the description of the likelihood of a specific action. Forgiveness is a fundamental experience. Fundamental, transcending cultures and eras.

When we forgive, we give new chances and get new opportunities. However, every person might not forgive another in the course of his life. We do not trust anymore. We do not believe that the other person will act again in the way we suspected "per se".

While interpersonal forgiveness is deeply individual, biographical, and situational, human beings are not only individuals but also part of communities. We are born into families, cultures, environments. In these "social systems" we are wanted and unwanted members. What our community does throws light on us as part of the Mueller family, as a German, or as an employee of company XY. We are ambassadors of a community—usually of countless numbers. What happens when we as individuals have "gambled away trust"? A thoughtless remark by a musician, an advantage taken by a politician, outrageously high bonus payments for a manager? Communities know "what is proper" and sanction violations of the unwritten rules. The public scandal is the communities' collective disappointment. But again, communities can forgive. Does our community give us "a second chance"? Who specifically forgives?

This book is about exploring what forgiveness is as a human gift. Which psychological and sociological prerequisites must not only be rationally understood but also individually emotionalized so that the process of forgiveness can begin. As an individual act, but above all in terms of community and individual. What does forgiveness mean and what basic understanding is possible with regard to what seems to be a "mysterious" human act? Why do we forgive—or not? Why is forgiveness so important for the functioning and safeguarding of communities?

Communities are social creatures. They want to be sure about themselves to exist and grow. They succeed by becoming aware of themselves. Nothing helps this as much as breaking the rules. Obviously, this is a deeply human condition. There is nothing you can do about it. But it is extremely exciting to deal with it for a moment.

1 What Does Collective Forgiveness Mean?

1.1 Prologue

In an age of all-encompassing rational pretensions, numbers, statistics, extrapolations, scenarios, roadmaps, and risk mitigation, there is a danger that phenomena that defy statistical, neurological, or empirical observation will be categorized as pseudoscientific hokum. For the most part, these purely measurable observations, though common, explain little. For it is thought upon, but not in anything.

The sciences of our day try to attribute almost all phenomena to numerical explanation parameters. A comprehensive quantification frenzy that knows no bounds. Biology, chemistry, and algorithms are integrated in order to penetrate and explain actions and emotions. In most cases, much seems plausible and comprehensible: Equipped with series of numbers, ratios, attitude- and emotional panels, and tracking tools, science can present ratio-based results in a predictable and traceable way within the "academic community" and sometimes even to a broad public. The use of indices is particularly pronounced in day-to-day economics. As economist and Gestalt sociologist Timm Homann described years ago: "Key figures may seem to arise from analytically sober motives, but everyone is familiar with the professional atmosphere that fills a conference room when numbers and their combinations are juggled as an unacceptable matter of course. Managers whose argumentation is based on this juggling art always prevail. Managers who argue on the supposedly softer parameters of 'smiling faces', 'continuous quality levels' and 'stylistic presentation of goods', i.e. who focus on corporate style in its complexity, are often considered unprepared and succumb in the decision-making process [...]" (Homann 2000, pp. 322–323).

In his reflections on the quantification of socio-psychological and sociological phenomena, the macro-sociologist Steffen Mau describes the mental effects:

"Numbers offer an—often very convincing—answer to our needs for objectification, object-relatedness, and rationalization. While numbers abstract from concrete social contexts, they are not just mathematics. Behind them are processes of value assignment, which give numbers a meaning or a 'value' in the first place. Quantifications can therefore be seen as manifest forms of attributing value, which is why it is not only the fact that quantification takes place that is interesting but also how and by whom" (Mau 2017, p. 29). In his further reflections, Mau points out that the will to quantify is directly related to the economization of all areas of life. This is because the focus on numerical parameters in complex dynamics and performances creates comparability, which leads individual actors into controllable competition for limited resources. This is even more important because an increasingly unmanageable environment demands that the attention of the individual can fall back on sources that simplify and summarize information. In a world of numbers, it is no longer about individuals with individual backgrounds and preconditions but about units that are backed by certain (better or worse) data parameters to create comparability.

Perpetual comparison is a general trait of human beings. Ensuring and creating a "positive self-image" is one of the most powerful psychological impulses. As "beings of difference" (Georg Simmel) we want to compare ourselves with others to determine and, if necessary, improve our position in the world - with all the good and bad effects on social interaction.

Quantifications guarantee systematized access and offer indicators of otherwise complex social phenomena. Thinking in numbers as an overarching blueprint seems to be a conditional prerequisite in order not to run the risk of arguing in categories of discarded metaphysics. Limiting the argumentation to cognitive processing of social phenomena on the basis of learned instruments and methods is status quo beyond science, but at least worthy of criticism.

The belief in an overarching explicability and plannability of all phenomena has become a principle of accelerated modernity. It reveals the desire for fixed parameters in a time without fundamental support and attachment. A parity psychosis prevails that attempts to reduce everything and everyone to homogeneous number-based indicators. Steffen Mau suspects the reasons lie in the economically induced zeitgeist: "Quantifications institutionalize certain 'orders of value' that provide us with standards of judgment and justifications about how things are to be seen and evaluated" (Mau 2017, p. 24). The cost of this is a focus on a one-dimensional, numbers-based worldview. However, this pays little attention to the essential "mechanics" of social organizations.

In his book "Complexity: The Emerging Science at the Edge of Order and Chaos (Inseln im Chaos)", physicist Mitchell Waldrop pointed out in relation to the study of complex systems that, unlike the natural sciences, social organizations are non-linear: "In physics, an elementary particle has no past, no experience, no goals, no future expectations. It simply is. That is why physicists can talk so freely about 'general laws': Their particles respond to forces with blind obedience. In economics, on the other hand, 'our particles have to think ahead and try to figure out how other particles might react if they behave in certain ways'" (Waldrop 1993, p. 175). In addition to this unpredictability, the very thought of chaos theory in nonlinear systems makes clear how even small events can have immense effects on an overall structure.

Enforced, classical claims often have in common to grasp a phenomenon on their surface, their countable and measurable manifestations, to make them tangible. Every person has fallen in love at some point (at least this is to be expected). Love means something profoundly different to people. But even love is not safe from quantification: For example, loosely based on the systems theorist Niklas Luhmann, love is a quotient of the frequency of communication between two people, which is more frequent at the beginning of getting to know each other than it is after 10 years of marriage, and after 20 years usually shows hardly any activity. This approach is superficially plausible, understandable, and correct in its moving logic. This approach is the basis of modernity and a majority, scientifically oriented worldview.

The processes of counting, measuring, structuring, systematizing have made progress possible and replaced diffuse beliefs and arbitrary truths. The inexorable mechanization and above all digitalization of all areas of life has made it possible at all that even the most personal areas—from the emotion scanner to fitness tracking to switching on the coffee machine, the light and the adequate music within the fully automated "smart home"—are now data-based. Reserves of digital freedom are becoming fewer and fewer and will probably disappear completely in the foreseeable future, as Dave Eggers dystopically describes in his novel "The Circle": "And then on top of that, he lived there all alone, in some hut. No wonder he gets depressed and spirals into a delusional paranoid state. […] People wanted to help. They tried to help. […] When you reject humanity, when you reject all the tools that are available to you, all the support that is available to you, bad things happen. When you reject the technology that prevents cars from crashing, you crash—physically. If you reject the help and love of billions of compassionate people in the world, you crash—emotionally" (Eggers 2014, pp. 525–526).

However, the rationalist-descriptive view embraces only one perspective. What is love in and of itself? Are we

1 What Does Collective Forgiveness Mean?

satisfied with a number, a quotient? Here, now begins the thinking and the search for knowledge from within. The "Nihil est in intellectu, quod non prius fuerit in sensibus—Nothing is in the intellect that was not previously in the senses" is indeed correct and describes an empirically-based view of the world but the philosopher and mathematician Gottfried Wilhelm Leibniz extended this sentence three centuries ago to include the exclamation "nisi intellectus ipse - except the intellect itself". So there is always logic in things, which - if the gain of knowledge is wanted all-embracingly - must likewise form a level of penetration.

One thing is clear: This deeper level promotes subjectivity, qualitative variables, estimates, assumptions, openness to interpretation, and thus errors, which, however, characterize precisely the things of life, and to a large extent even constitute them. Life means dealing with the uncertain, sometimes even with the epistemic abyss. Or as the German scholar, Jürgen Wertheimer puts it: "Anyone who sets out to establish unambiguity by means of shallow positivist thinking not only falls short, but also eliminates any thinking in terms of possibilities" (Wertheimer 2020, p. 59).

Against this background, it is possible to try to break love down to quantifications, but it contradicts the (doomed) attempt to isolate a complex overall picture. Thus, Peter Sloterdijk describes love against the background of his epistemological interest with a diametrically opposed explanatory approach: "According to Plato, the binding forces that work between lovers go back to a homesickness for the totality, the traces of which point to the prehistory of the great couple. Like all mythical wholes, the round self-sufficient primordial man is subject to the dramaturgical triple act of imperfection, the catastrophe of separation, and restoration" (Sloterdijk 1998, p. 213). What is at stake here is not quantifiable contacts, but an understanding of the energies of action and dynamics. Only the consideration of both aspects enables a systemic clarification.

Love cannot be explained monocausally, it eludes rationality and unambiguous prediction. Assuming an inner perspective, numerous different aspects of innumerable actors and levels act on each other, overarching, interpenetrating, and adapting with the result that certain behavior can never be predicted with absolute certainty. What remains possible, however, is the prediction of certain probabilities with regard to a state of affairs, a constellation, an activity. It can be explained why people act in a certain way, what moves them and makes them act in a self-active way.

The following thoughts are, thus, about the attempt of a scientifically-founded way of looking at the inner view. The search for the "great whole", which the Norwegian novelist Karl Ove Knausgard succinctly formulates in his sixth volume under the title "Fighting": "We have eliminated all thoughts about the great and all thoughts about the authentic. We live in a sea of things and spend much of our waking time in front of screens. […] The longing for reality, the longing for authenticity are nothing but an expression of a longing for meaning, and meaning grows out of contexts, out of how we are connected to each other and to our environment" (Knausgard 2018, pp. 687–688).

What might help us in our search? An old way of looking at things: The analysis of the inner view can be effectively brought together under the term "Gestalt". At the latest after World War 2, the notion of a "Gestalt" hardly played a role in the social scientific study of facts. The Gestalt sociologist Alexander Deichsel points out that the "Gestalt" as a variable of observation and non-interchangeable unit of cultural systems was intensively worked on in the German-speaking world by authors such as Alfred Vierkandt, Wolfgang Köhler, and Walther Schering (cf. Deichsel 1997,

p. 389). Schering himself defined the Gestalt approach in relation to groups as follows: "The social group is a Gestalt, i.e. a whole in which what happens on the part is determined according to the inner laws of this whole; the social group thus forms the founding unit in social events" (cited in Deichsel 1997, p. 409).

Even if we resist, we are not free from a "world view of number"—it conditions our search for knowledge. All these, however, are trifles of thought in view of the possibilities that a view from within makes possible. If this claim does not always succeed, the readership may also forgive the author. As the saying goes: Many are right, but few are true. And if few true were depicted here, then it would already be a large amount.

1.2 No Forgiveness Without Freedom

The subject of this slim book, collective forgiveness as a thought and action of human communication, is in no way inferior to love in its mysteriousness. Why do we forgive some people and not others? Why cannot we forgive right away? Why have people always forgiven each other - or rejected the very act of forgiving? Do we forgive individuals in our environment more easily or more difficult than a group of people? And above all: Why does collective forgiveness exist everywhere and since time immemorial?

A look back: Georg Simmel, one of the founding fathers of German social science, described forgiveness as a human characteristic that was not "quite comprehensible". He was to be proved right over 100 years later. In recent years, psychologists, sociologists, philosophers, and theologians, in particular, have grappled with this very incomprehensibility and attempted to understand the individual driving forces. The diversity of fields of work and points of view has not only created diverse unconnected views but has also generated small-scale judgments that view forgiveness primarily in terms of its regulative effects and do not focus on the seemingly diffuse causal level, refer to the structural inner workings of the processes.

It is all the more important to understand this great feeling and action in its deep structure and to link it to current considerations. It is, therefore, necessary to explore the approach of groups towards individuals—especially when a person has fallen into collective disgrace.

In a hyper-complex world where certain expectations of action and performance are crucial every day to enable smooth functioning, there is a need for mechanisms that can restore the connectivity of actions even in the face of conflict. What is "the ultimate reason" (Ernst Jünger) for grasping fragments and splinters of the great mosaic that embraces and sustains human interaction. As individuals, we are at the same time actors within groups into which we are integrated without thinking: As German, European, Berliner, Hamburger, football fan, employee, father or mother, allotment enthusiast, Catholic or atheist. Man's capacity for culture is inexhaustible—even global standardization through information technology, world trade, and borderless manufacturing and transport technology may not fundamentally reduce the reference to existing cultural patterns. These groups or social systems structure our lives and shape and condition our thinking and feeling.

The philosopher Peter Sloterdijk points to the contemporary fundamental conflict between I and we and takes a critical view of the idea of a delimited I: "Where such individualisms appear, one can conclude with a high degree of psychological evidence that there is a basic neurotic position of freedom; it is characteristic of this that a subject cannot think of itself as contained, limited, embraced and occupied. It is the basic neurosis of occidental culture to have to dream of a subject that observes, names, possesses everything without letting itself be contained, named, possessed by anything [...]" (Sloterdijk 1998, p. 85). Elsewhere, Sloterdijk expresses himself even more vehemently with regard to the self-perception of late-modern societies: "They declare themselves to be cases of a statistical averageness that rig themselves up individualistically" (Sloterdijk 2005, p. 138).

In his reflections on late modernity, the sociologist Andreas Reckwitz diagnoses that a structural change is taking place that is replacing standardization with the "logic of the special" in all areas of life (cf. Reckwitz 2017, p. 11). This specialness encompasses the search for the unique, the authentic, and the extraordinary. Reckwitz refers to this as "singularisation". Since the 1970s and 1980s, he argues, a dynamic has been developing that involves the realization of this aspiration at all levels of the society: "Singularized are certainly also, but by no means only human subjects, which is why the classical concept of individuality reserved for humans no longer fits. Singularization also encompasses, and to a very special degree, the fabrication and appropriation of things and objects. It affects the design and perception of spaces as well as temporalities and, not least, collectives" (Reckwitz 2017, p. 12).

Authenticity and particularity on the one hand and standardization and collectivity on the other - is there not a contradiction discernible here? The solution of modernity is profoundly creative: The processes of particularity are highly standardized in themselves ("machinic standardization"), they are socially desired, anchored and form the coordinate system in which individual behavior receives its norms and fixed points and internalizes them as "second nature" ("infrastructures of particularity" Reckwitz 2017, p. 73). The groupness of social processes does not dissolve in late modernity either; it embodies itself in a different variant. What remains decisive is the idea that human beings continue to think, act, live in the conventions and overarching cultural techniques.

The collective human being has therefore not changed but at best the characteristics and personalizations have become finer and more detailed. Every human being not only wants to participate in the world but also to take part in it: He makes the things of this world his own. People seek proximity to what is actually distant, the connection to epochs and events that have long since passed or lie in the distant future - simultaneity in non-simultaneity. Not every place arouses identical desires for all people, but only those things that are special in some detail have the potential to occupy our imaginary world and thus become part of our history, our personality. Yet the special is always concrete: It consists of buildings, people, animals, landscapes, or a style. Even things can be home. The prerequisite: Their message character is uniform, homogeneous, shared in terms of content so that it is understood at all and fulfills its orientation function.

What applies to the world of things and services can also be applied to the forms of social conventions and actions. Even if modern socialities are splitting up into ever smaller milieus with their respective cultures of action, the fundamental techniques of social interaction remain. Mass continues to exist in an infinite plural these days - whether it is personalized cereal, the individual children's picture book, the holiday trip, or the free-to-view Netflix program. Even "collective forgiveness" is subject to social conventions and dramaturgies, i.e. the way groups punish and sanction moral transgressions - self-similarly adapted to the zeitgeist and independent of legal violations.

1 What Does Collective Forgiveness Mean?

The crucial question arises: Can groups forgive individuals even though their morality has been questioned, ignored, or willingly transgressed? This is not a clear-cut decision in the sense of a judgment, but above all the question of an organic reintegration as part of a community. Is there collective forgiveness? Is the idea of a collective forgiveness real at all, or is it a theoretical wish because the indissoluble condition of forgiveness is precisely deeply personal forgiveness between two or very few people - Hannah Ahrendt, in her reflections on forgiveness as a political category, first wrote of an interpersonal process. Can this contradiction be resolved by the sociological concept of quasi-persons, hyperorganisms (Ferdinand Tönnies), which are effective as social facts (Max Weber)?

As yet, except in theories of political conflict resolution following war or civil war crimes, there is little consideration of a theory of collective forgiveness from an internal perspective. The supposedly small triggers for collective forgiveness, the football player who disappoints his fans, the politician who attaches undeserved merit to himself or accepts inappropriate attentions, the musician who listlessly delivers his concerts, the lecturer who makes a tomboyish remark in the lecture hall, the television presenter, who does not question his guests respectfully ... all transgressions, small or somewhat larger public disturbances, which are legally insignificant, or are not punishable at all, or only marginally so, but which interest us and public opinion enormously, and which we sometimes take note of painfully or only amusedly. For the "accused" of a diffuse, intangible but immensely effective instance, public opinion, these just perceived transgressions have grave consequences: Withdrawal from office, resignation from the public stage, erosion of followership, or a media drumfire of disapproval, and with it social ostracism: The losing, the violation, the (imagined) expulsion from the community. For good? Usually only for a short time. What happens when a "fallen man" strives back into the public eye? How is he forgiven, do the structural "de-guilt hurdles" follow specific patterns?

The following pages provide a look at this "enigmatic" feeling and its general manifestations. In doing so, it is useful to first look at what "forgiveness" as an action entails, but more importantly, what "forgiveness" means for groups or—formulated in a somewhat more social-psychological way—for social alliance systems. Therefore, terms like group, alliance, community, and public opinion are key to better understand collective forgiveness.

Above all, the notion of a "public opinion" seems useful and fruitful as an explanatory approach to the dynamics of collective forgiveness: More than 100 years ago, the forefather of German social science, Ferdinand Tönnies, described this "subject of opinions" as a structurer with a clear structure of command and prohibition and self-observable actors who formulate and demand a public opinion for themselves. In his book "Kritik der Öffentlichen Meinung" he defines: "[…] for public opinion, the subject is an essentially, especially politically, connected totality, which has agreed to think and judge in this way, and which, precisely because of this, belongs as if by itself to the public sphere, to public life. This brings us close to a strong difference in the meaning of "to mean" itself. There it has predominantly a sense of thought (intellectualist), here predominantly a sense of will (voluntarist)" (Tönnies 2002, p. 159).

Integrating Tönnies' thoughts into the analysis of "forgiveness" could be a valuable key to understanding this incomprehensible feeling a little more clearly. This is difficult, because the social will-form of public opinion, however shaped, is first of all an imagined assembly. It defies clear empirical measurability. Ferdinand Tönnies expressed this in the following words: "Here, however, public opinion is essentially a will, will in judgment and by judgment - the judgment, however, is a unitary act—consequently a conscious and expressed form of will, after the manner of the resolution which a court of justice or otherwise a 'decidable' assembly 'takes', on which it agrees—an expression of the will of a totality, which, however, is not assembled as an audience or subject of public opinion, except in spirit—as a rule, much too large to be imagined as an assembly" (Tönnies 2002, p. 159).

Forgiveness places the value system of a group in the context of evaluation and assessment. Its ambivalence is obvious: On the one hand, a community assures itself of known and approved customs, procedures, and unwritten rules but, on the other hand, the transgression also makes structural breaks and difficulties in the realization of these very specifications clear—the consensus is in danger and the sanction has the task of punishing and penalizing them in order to force a self-assurance of the group beyond the individual case. In other words: Every violation of rules weakens and strengthens an overall system in equal measure. Weakens, because breaks and contradictions become apparent—up to the point of breaking off and adapting these very rules to the times. Strengthens, because in the ideal case this breaking of rules clarifies and revitalizes the rules across the board. Because personal misdemeanors or transgressions have a direct impact on the respective community against the background of the "human social system".

Collective forgiveness is, thus, one of the decisive mechanisms in complex organizations that ensure the social action structure. The learned law recedes in favor of a social act of renunciation (usually also due to a lack of punishment-related evidence). A final judgment is not expected, may not even be pronounced, in order to enable a quick possibility of connection. The legal verdict and the serving of a sentence also differ fundamentally from personal forgiveness: A legal verdict of guilt does not ask for a personal admission of guilt. The punishment is formally finished at some point. Forgiveness, on the other hand, requires insight and foresight. In other words, forgiveness means the future.

Literature

Deichsel A (1997) Marke als Gestaltsystem. In: Brandmeyer K, Deichsel A (eds) Jahrbuch Markentechnik 1997/98. Deutscher Fachverlag, Frankfur, Germany

Eggers D (2014) Der circle. Kiepenheuer & Witsch, Köln, Germany

Homann T (2000) Die Marke als Instanz der strategischen Unternehmensführung. Dissertation, Universität Hamburg

Knausgard KO (2018) Kämpfen. btb, München

Mau S (2017) Das metrische Wir. Über Quantifizierung des Sozialen. Suhrkamp, Berlin, Germany

Reckwitz A (2017) Die Gesellschaft der Singularitäten. Suhrkamp, Berlin, Germany

Sloterdijk P (1998) Blasen. Suhrkamp, Frankfurt, Germany

Sloterdijk P (2005) Im Weltinnenraum des Kapitals. Suhrkamp, Frankfurt, Germany

Tönnies F (2002) Kritik der öffentlichen Meinung. Walter de Gruyter, Berlin, Germany

Waldrop MM (1993) Inseln im Chaos. Die Erforschung komplexer Systeme. Rowohlt, Reinbek, Germany

Wertheimer J (2020) Europa. Geschichte seiner Kulturen. Pinguin, München, Germany

2

About Favor and Autonomy

What are the prerequisites for forgiveness? Forgiveness only becomes necessary when a person's behavior generates resonance, that is, is perceived by a counterpart—as beneficial, obstructive, perhaps even destructive. Perspective about impact, however, is deeply subjective. And yet, beyond an individual's perception, there seem to be instances or "hyperorganic living beings " that go beyond cultural custom to classify individual actions and determine dos and don'ts. Between freedom, discipline, and sanctioning, we test our role as individuals and social beings.

2.1 The Starting Point: The Freedom of Error

The world is full.

Full of possibilities, ways, and options. The world is full of thoughts, considerations, and decisions. The world is a place of unlimited ideas and plans. And at the same time: One thought not thought out, one scenario not "played out" and already the one, the decisive chance of life might be forfeited. If I decide for this one woman, this one man as a life partner, then I decide at the same time against 4 billion others. Do I choose this profession, this job, this holiday resort, this house, this doctor, this product? The choice is freedom—and uncertainty. Omnis determinatio est negatio—Every determination means exclusion, wrote the philosopher and mathematician Gottfried Wilhelm Leibniz at the beginning of the Enlightenment and clarifies the dilemma of freedom.

Today, the world is even more uncertain, even newer, and even more dissociated. Heaven has been brought down to earth. The price is that there is only one chance of paradise. Afterlife is over.

The fervent hunt for expanding boundaries and innovation seems all-encompassing: What is significant is what is new … and the new becomes more and more every day and ever more feverish in its novelty. Acceleration makes things blurred, almost unrecognizable. Everything is racing: Information, knowledge, paradigms, identities, orientations, habits, everything is subject to the relevance test in the now, is discarded, rethought. History, once the supreme discipline of the social sciences, is degenerating into a minor subject. Institutions, anchored structures, value orientations, and historical contexts are attacked and disappear. Perish. Exist only for a time.

Who remembers what the lead news on the daytime news was yesterday? Who remembers the social issues in 2016? What did I do for my 35th birthday? Our age is characterized by comprehensive restlessness at all levels (cf. Crary 2014, p. 16). In his remarks on acceleration, sociologist Hartmut Rosa makes it clear that a crucial imperative of modernity, against the backdrop of its capitalist ethic, is to use time resources as intensively as possible and thus to exploit them. This "basic experience of modernity" shapes a comprehensive need for action and thus the fear of constantly missing out on something, so that the "good life" passes one by (cf. Rosa 2005). A way out of life that integrates everything as far as possible - now and quickly. Carpe diem! Looking at the display of the smartphone, even during a tete-a-tete in a restaurant, illustrates our unconscious search for possible social connections while we are—in itself—(firmly) bound to an analog constellation.

The world is full.

The infinity of options, leveled by the ideal of the untenable twenty-first century: Freedom. Freedom is an imagined possibility. Fought for in global emancipatory conflicts and processes, in the awareness and autonomy of the self, often aspired to and not realized, successful life is measured—before a Western perspective—by the degree of individual sovereignty. Superficially, man has never seemed so free in action, but above all in thought. Supposedly freed of communal shackles—family, milieu, upbringing, even biological dispositions—we go our "own" way. More than 2000 years *after* its formulation, "Know Thyself" has not without reason become a popular calendar aphorism.

2.2 Freedom Creates Exclusion

Regardless of the actual degree of freedom in the sense of the variance of thoughts and life cliffs, at the same time, it has never been easier to make mistakes or to perceive decisions as mistakes in retrospect. And even this sensation is due to freedom, a freedom that allows for personal interpretation. For mistakes are possible when there is a choice. Freedom presupposes our ability not only to think of reality differently but to decide independently. Consciously, but also instinctively, as aesthetic judgment guides, urges, and shapes us. A relentless thought and impulse that often, all too often, pushes the sensible, rational self into the background and makes people act "quite rashly" and lustfully.

But this power of imagination and action is not a stable ground but at the same time an endless abyss. Mistakes are based on being able to commit between different possibilities. Determining a path and sometimes realizing that it could have gone differently or realizing that the decision chosen was wrong. This is the perplexing anarchy of our everyday lives. Acting and thinking as risk.

And at the same time, this supposed "wrong" of every decision shows us that there ought to be a "right". The ambiguity of a "wrong" only creates a cognition that seeks to circumvent it. But what is right in a world of comprehensibly many truths? Having overcome the dogmatism of a single correct social, political or religious worldview, we wrestle with the question of what might be absolute, at least individually—now and in the future. Knowingly with the realization that what seemed right before might turn out to be wrong over time. An infinitely radical disenchantment of all levels of reality and time. Oswald Spengler pointed out a good 100 years ago that the modern idea of duration is a very new one: "In ancient cities, nothing reminds us of duration, of the past, of what is to come, no reverently tended ruin, no work preconceived for generations yet unborn, no material chosen with significance despite technical difficulties. […] There is no 'time'" (Spengler 1986, p. 173). And in another place even more clearly: "All that is ordered is transient"(Spengler 1986, p. 217). If there is no extension of existing realities, it is easier to believe in a present order of "right" and "wrong," since it must be thought in the now alone.

Truth is—according to a Platonic understanding - when it makes man act "truthfully" and brings him close to the "good" by orienting to the facts: Makes man better, limits the instinctuality, the effects—in favor of an insightful weighing. Allowing distance from one's thoughts and actions. "Not good" is when people do not know or do not want to know, give themselves unreservedly to their impulses, excitements, and passions. Hermetically sealing off a reflection on oneself. This requires looking up from the display of one's smartphone - perhaps one will then see oneself in the switched-off black of the mini-screen.

However, the idea of what this "true" is changes permanently and at a faster pace. What is true fades or disintegrates because the social fixed points of these "truths" are themselves up for disposition. As evolving, learning, experiencing beings, whose actions are not exclusively drive-led but primarily self-directed, we condition this dynamic. The sociality that suddenly brands what was just "right" as "wrong". We may want but all this comes at the price of total uncertainty. The almost forgotten anthropologist Arnold Gehlen wrote: "Willing is the primordial phenomenon of man himself" (Gehlen 1962, p. 394). Will, he said, is constitutive of being human. For man, according to Gehlen, is "essentially willing." To assert self-will against nature is the perennial impulse. As agents, we are a conscious part of changing, interpretable possibilities.

2.3 The "Social Being" Human Being

However, these wills do not take place in isolation. The single will, the individual decision meets countless other decisions of directly or indirectly connected people. They stand in a fine network of desires, hopes, and needs that are interdependent - sometimes consciously, mostly covertly, even unnoticed by ourselves: Supporting or hindering. In this web of desires, alliances and discord occur—with others or sometimes with ourselves, delayed: The bad conscience as an imagined court of law, how the action should be: "Actually, I should have …" It is this notion of "right" and "wrong" that continues to structure our actions and makes us realize that complementing Gehlen, human beings are not only essentially volitional but also a "social being," a "zoon politikon," as Aristotle called it 3000 years ago. Sigmund Freund called these beacons of collective thought the "superego".

The step from the private to the public is quick: The moment a third person joins a conversation in private, society, the social, emerges. The social as a marketplace in which the individual joins with others or turns away from others. Founded in association with others' perspectives of connectedness: Shared volition regarding a goal, task, or solution. Previously completely independent people come together in some aspect of their actions: As fans of a football club, as Germans or Italians, as employees of a company, as car drivers or cyclists, as mothers or fathers. Man becomes part of imagined pre-connections, groups, sociotopes, which direct his actions and thinking in guard rails and predetermine his actions mostly without conscious willful decision. The social arises in different depths and characteristics.

According to the founder of German sociology, Ferdinand Tönnies, the social is subject to a fundamental condition: It must be willed. The mere and undirected coexistence of people does not yet exhibit a social quality. Sociality arises when it is lived together and when ideas and goals bring people into a supportive relationship with others: Social comes into being when people condition each other in a positive, supportive way. In his book "Gemeinschaft und Gesellschaft" (1887), Tönnies writes clearly: "This theory will be directed exclusively to the relations of mutual affirmation as to the objects of its investigation" (Tönnies 1991, p. 3).

The socio-economist and Gestalt philosopher Alexander Deichsel describes "the social" in this context as follows: "[…] that people affirmatively support and help each other in some way, that is, relate positively to each other and intentionally establish a relationship of mutual help" (Deichsel 1987, p. 95). It is crucial that the content of this relationship is not subject to a normative understanding but has a coherence of content.

What does this mean? Whether the goals of the agents are "social" in the colloquial understanding, i.e. philanthropically "good", is irrelevant for the consideration of the social. The concept of the social is neutral with respect to content: Against this background, a community of criminals can also be exceedingly social as a group, even if the results of their actions outside this group would be profoundly destructive and harmful.

Regardless of whether it is a matter of philanthropic or egoistic goals, a context of expectation and obligation emerges which reduces or channels the exclusively individual driving forces in the sense of the group. A supra-personal whole emerges from the individual wills, a specific body of wills that is primarily effective subconsciously and makes us, for example, be quiet in a church, enliven "good manners" in a conversation with a superior, and make us choose a certain wardrobe for special occasions—in these moments specific culture acts in us. Tönnies described these "cultures" as follows: "In this sense, living units of people living together cannot only be compared to organisms but are rightly thought of and understood as hyper-organic living beings" (Tönnies 1981, p. 4.).

The characteristic of these subjects is not only expansion but presence in the reality of life, not only movement but direction and goal, not dynamism but gestalt-like momentum. It is obvious that not every network is characterized by a similar depth and compression: The relationship between mother, father, and children (hopefully) has a different intensity than to the gas station attendant (if he still exists), the cashier in the supermarket and to the dentist—nevertheless, according to the access described, they are hyper-organisms that are effective in two ideal-typical forms: Communities and in societies—they will be described below.

The moment people form a community, a state of detachment arises at the same time. The turning towards one's own or chosen is automatically and completely without bad intentions the turning away from everything else: When we shake hands with one person, we turn our backs on all others—faces become backs. The fact that we come together in communities creates an unmanageable number of alliances that include some and exclude others. You cannot advance anything good in this world without it excluding, keeping out, rejecting others. Since man, as a social being, seeks interaction with others, since it is, as it were, inherent in him as a human disposition, the perception of exclusion leads to the effect of forming group alliances in other constellations: When the whole world allies itself, we do not want to be outside and become part of other communities, and indeed of those that welcome us or that we even create ourselves as family, entrepreneurs or athletes. So, the perception of exclusion keeps the flywheel of alliance-building constantly turning: Exclusion creates containment. The social horizon is infinitely stretched in its manifestations and variations—exclusion creates containment.

The "social" as a relationship of different wills to each other is a reality of life. However, people do not relate to each other as isolated individuals, but we are carriers of accumulated imprints, experiences, and connections that "make us typical", locate and guide us. The discussion is old, ancient: What makes, what shapes the person? His talents, charisms, or the social context? According to Karl Marx, being creates consciousness. Or rather: Consciousness creates being?

Despite neurological research, finely branched studies, and in-depth interviews, the answer remains multifaceted. A definitive weighting or even an either-or does not exist. In scientific observation, a mixed form has been agreed upon. Life is not an ideal type—pure and without contradictions—but complex, diverse, and unpredictable. The uncertainties, the possibilities, the options are what makes human beings human.

It seems clear that people are never context-free actors but are part of and members of countless social macro- and micro-systems. It is not we who steer but things that steer in us. Not we control a language but a language controls us - otherwise, communication would not be possible. The social arises through the sharing of experiences. The "sharing" multiplies our knowledge with others. Sharing brings us together because it requires exchange and understanding.

In his studies, Sigmund Freud elaborates the fundamentals of this phenomenon in a concise and lively manner. A mental furioso: "Each individual is a component of many masses, bound in many ways by identification, and has built up his ego-ideal according to the most diverse models. Each individual thus has a share in many mass souls, in that of his race, class, religious community, statehood, etc., and can, moreover, raise himself to a measure of independence and orginality" (Freud 2000, p. 815).

Against the backdrop of increasingly uniform world culture, i.e. consumer culture, which levels the diversity of the world and realities of life with the help of a digital cloud at the expense of "small happiness", Freud's thoughts have never been more relevant than they are today.

2.4 Social Living Beings: Existent, but Not Tangible

It is these gestalt systems, these "imagined" social living beings, "hyperorganisms" (according to Ferdinand Tönnies) in contrast to biological organisms, which are neither tangible nor clearly delimitable but which structure, direct and guides life with fundamental force, in that we are part of "the Germans", "the motorists", "the Catholics", "the Schmidt family": No one has ever shaken hands with Germany, no one knows to whom he would have to write a letter if he wanted to address "the motorists." And yet our ordered life is based on thinking in precisely these categories. Tönnies formulated this insight in the following words: "In this sense, living units of people living together cannot only be compared to organisms but are rightly thought of and understood as *hyper-organic living beings*" (Tönnies 1981, p. 4). Crucial is the notion of a super-personal will that is inherent in a social organism: The members of such a hyper-organic living being constitute as a community a will of their own, which, even if it is not completely uniform, is characterized by certain classifications of reality and forms a type and structure towards the outside.

More recently, there is a parallel to these thoughts with the theory of memes developed and much discussed by the biologist Richard Dawkins. Memes are mechanisms of inheritance of ideas (memes as cultural elements that are passed on primarily as language and through imitation), in analogy to genes as carriers of physiological predispositions (cf. Blackmore 2000). The Israeli historian Juval Harari has portrayed these strange but omnipresent (idea) creatures succinctly in his book "A Brief History of Time": "Every large-scale human enterprise—from an archaic tribe to an ancient city to a medieval church or a modern state—is firmly rooted in shared histories that exist only in the minds of men. […] These things, however, exist only in the stories we humans invent and tell each other. Gods, nations, money, human rights, and laws do not even exist— they exist only in our collective imaginations" (Harari 2015, p. 41).

Georg Simmel, a sociological classic from today's perspective, already made it clear a good 100 years ago that the degree of differentiation of culture was recognizable by the fact that the number of hyperorganisms, the "social circles", was constantly increasing: While the people of middle age were anchored in a manageable number of cultural carriers, the sum of these action fields has grown to a number that can hardly be documented. We wake up in the morning, are residents of a city, tenants of an apartment, listeners to a certain radio station, customers of a spread, train riders, employees … to describe only a fraction of the "memberships" that structure, if not accompany, our day. Digitalization has increased participation in the world and its possibilities to infinity via the Internet, we can network globally with people who engage in the identical pastime, have the same last names, order products from all parts of the world and, even if we are spending the evening in a group with friends, be somewhere else entirely with a constant sideways glance and a swipe on the display of a smartphone: "Still in mechanical repetition, however, there remains a glimmer of what we know to be a deceptive hope that one more click or touch could redeem us from overwhelming monotony" (Crary 2014, p. 75).

Man is involved in his power of decision for or against a community but he is self-determined and free in his aesthetic (liking) judgment. No human being can dictate to another human being what kind of music he will find beautiful. Nothing has yet become known of prescribing a favorite color. This one-woman we love, although everything speaks against it. The spread of bread tastes us or also not - coaxing does not help. We can "over-convince", i.e. bear witness to our assessments and feelings and hope that this will meet with a response, that the assessments will be appreciated and that they will spill over to the opposite pole. Nevertheless, the judgment of liking is not subject to any causal logic. It is the only free judgment of man and it is in its expression and quality precisely the characteristic that conditions the decisively human in the first place.

There is no automatism with regard to the orientation of our preferences. Those who grew up in a village do not automatically have to live in a village themselves; perhaps it is precisely this life experience that leads to the city as a place of residence (although the probability is rather lower and becomes even lower at the latest when a family is founded). The fact that our insights and affections are culturally and biographically underpinned does not imply that they are fixed in content. Perhaps experiences lead us precisely to no longer desire this experienced and to specifically decide against it. Whatever aesthetically founded attraction exists and in its combination gives rise to the individual, the least, in fact, nothing, we have thought up or created ourselves. It is the combination of what is already there that makes us unique.

As a result, this means that the human being is always part of something. Equipped with this mantle of overarching interconnectedness, the human being enters into relationships with others and, in the interplay of individual goals, creates "social" as a conducive and profoundly creative interaction.

As twenty-first-century humans, the notion of limited individuality may irritate us, perhaps even offend our sense of self but enlightenment, democracy, the welfare state, Netflix, configuration programs, Spotify are only standardized pseudo-options-givers, played-out possibilities, against the backdrop of several thousand years of basic laws of human emotion.

2.5 The Judgment of Liking as a Social Category

In 1925, the French philosopher Maurice Halbwachs published his study "Memory and its Social Conditions" [*Les Cadres sociaux de la mémoire*]- still a major work of collective identity research today. The main thesis of his observations is that personal memory, i.e. individuality, does not derive from previous dispositions but is to a large extent socially conditioned. Halbwachs summarizes this fact with the idea of the so-called "cadres sociaux" ("social frameworks"). It is this "social framework" that puts people in a position to ensure the connectivity of communication. The communication researcher Astrid Erll describes this fundamental thesis in the following words: "Man is a social being. Without other people, he is denied access not only to such clearly collective phenomena as language or customs but […] also to his memory" (Erll 2005, p. 15).

Because human beings grow up in this social order, internalize it and learn it as a means of communication, their perception, interpretation, and classification are to a large extent based on collective determinations. Halbwachs writes: "There would be, in this sense, a collective memory and a social frame of memory, and our individual thought would be capable of remembering to the extent that it kept within and participated in this frame of reference" (Halbwachs 1985, p. 21). This means: There is no individual memory that is not socially grounded.

The individualization of the human being takes place through the numerous systems or - in a different conceptualization - organizations in which he moves: Thus, a human being is a member of a family, a milieu, a religion, and a nation, among others. These so-called "outlook points" (Halbwachs) feed the human being with a multitude of different social frameworks, which in their combination constitute a unique psyche. The contents are homogeneous; the combinatorics create uniqueness. The contents of these outlook points are passed on or socially inherited in different ways - almost exclusively informally. For this reason, man, his thinking and feeling are not the same. It is highly differentiated, peculiar, and eludes absolute prognosis.

A prerequisite for the emergence of collective identities lies in the continuous interactions of the individual actors with each other: "The individual calls up his memories with the help of the frames of reference of social memory" (Halbwachs 1985, p. 381). Cultural contents that are not part of everyday life, that do not show repetition, are not only lost individually but at the same time, the group as a group is neither consolidated nor stabilized. The reassurance of "one's own stories", which condense into customs, seems to be constitutive for the strength of individual identity.

2.6 Life in Chaos

Where does this lead? What does this mean for our interaction and perspective on the other? Everyday life is a self-chosen and self-induced thunderstorm of succeeding and failing possibilities. Everyday life is confusing … in all fields. Everyday life is a decision … based on experience. Everyday life is weighing … in fractions of a second.

In the wild staccato of the accelerated zeitgeist, everyday life means not only producing countless information and messages but also—this is their purpose—processing them, evaluating them, and finally transforming them into actions. Over and over again, we have to decide: T-shirt or sweater, suit or jeans, car or train, house or apartment, Coke or Pepsi, French fries or salad, BMW or Dacia, buy or rent, Catholic or Buddhist, Germany or Europe, single or couple, Elena or Maria, Jürgen or Andreas … some decisions affect our entire life, others only the midday meal. We choose with the intention to be "right", to meet our wishes, preferences, demands, or to bring them in line with controlling guidelines.

Sometimes a person fails with this desire to others, against others, all too often also the self-image. But the assessment of the results of our decisions and life works can lead to a positive or negative judgment—depending on the point of view, depending on which phase of life we are in. What is clear is: In addition to the obvious "drama of freedom" as an individual category, the possibility of choosing different options has an impact not only on the individual but also on others.

The personally advantageous decision may have positive or negative consequences for a person involved. Freedom requires union, alliance building but also disharmony, sometimes even dispute and quarrel. Modern man must increasingly orient himself to himself—religion or customs no longer help, certainly not absolutely. This self is not completely defined, it is not pre-given but only given up—every human being must ceaselessly weigh and make his individual decisions by reflection, examination, action.

The fact of wanting leads to the question: What is right? What meets the subjective wishes, expectations, plans? What corresponds to one's own goals? Do individual goals harm others?

Freedom creates not only the personally assessable possibility of success and failure but also a social context in which subjective action is judged. What happens in a world, i.e. in a social structure, when failure, failing, and failing to succeed are not only possible but inevitable due to infinite diversity? Yes, in that it is not even clear when failure occurs at all? Failure can, therefore—depending on the group-specific perspective—mean success at the same time because the assessment is subject to solely subjective and thus relative frames of reference: Individual people, but also communities. This means that the assessment itself takes place on two levels: An individual and a social one.

Accordingly, social interaction is not the only individual but structurally an alternation between fulfillment and disappointment. That which we perceive as good and right may hurt another person - sometimes one is not possible without the other.

In effect, the perpetual automatism of "success and failure" could lead to both actors irretrievably abandoning their communication, an experience once made ending the discourse for the time being. However, the reality of life proves that people re-establish their communication despite the opposing effects of a decision. Forgiveness makes the maintenance of social interactions formally straightforward and pragmatic, i.e., without flanking organizations. A world in which people are networked with other people as never before, and in which communication and conflict are thus possible, would not be vital and exchangeable in the long term without forgiveness—forgiveness thus requires connectivity beyond a dispute.

The individual perspective, i.e. forgiveness as an interaction between two people (one forgives the other) has been studied many times in the past as a theological, philosophical and psychological issue. Forgiveness as a subcategory of forgiveness moves the behavior close to religious actions and traditions. Here, however, the question is how a "public" forgives an individual. So how does the social interaction of forgiveness work from hyper-organism to organism? How do these "things in people's heads" (Harari) communicate with the individual and make them part of something or else exclude them? The aim is to describe the dynamics and determinants of collective forgiveness.

It seems as if delimitable phases and levels of activity work, provided that the social misbehaviour of a member of a group is socially compensated and finally leads again to overlapping acceptance.

Literature

Blackmore S (2000) Die Macht der Meme oder Die Evolution von Kultur und Geist: oder Die Evolution von Kultur und Geist, vol 2010. Spektrum

Crary J (2014) Schlaflos im Spätkapitalismus. Wagenbach, Berlin

Deichsel A (1987) Von Tönnies her gedacht. Soziologische Skizzen. Rolf Fechner Verlag, Hamburg, Germany

Erll A (2005) Kollektives Gedächtnis und Erinnerungskulturen. Metzler, Stuttgart, Germany

Freud S (2000) Massenpsychologie und Ich-Analyse, IX edn. Fischer, Frankfurt, Germany

Gehlen A (1962) Der Mensch. Seine Natur und seine Stellung in der Welt. Athenäum Verlag, Frankfurt, Germany

Halbwachs M (1985) Das Gedächtnis und seine sozialen Bedingungen. Suhrkamp, Frankfurt, Germany

Harari YN (2015) Eine kurze Geschichte der Menschheit. Pantheon, München, Germany

Rosa H (2005) Beschleunigung. Die Veränderung der Zeitstrukturen in der Moderne. Suhrkamp, Frankfurt, Germany

Spengler O (1986) Der Untergang des Abendlandes. Umrisse einer Morphologie der Weltgeschichte. dtv, München

Tönnies F (1981) Einführung in die Soziologie. Enke, Stuttgart, Germany

Tönnies F (1991) Gemeinschaft und Gesellschaft. Grundbegriffe der Reinen Soziologie. Wissenschaftliche Buchgesellschaft, Darmstadt, Germany

3

About Forgiveness

The "cultural career" of forgiveness has existed since humans first met. We forgive all the time—in small contexts and fundamental life decisions: Sometimes it is the stranger who steps on our foot on the subway ("It's ok!") to the close friend who betrayed our blind trust ("You hurt me immensely, but we'll try …"). To understand how "forgiveness" works, it makes sense to trace the evolution of the meaning of the term and to show what rational and emotional aspects characterize forgiveness as an action between two people but also between a person and a group.

3.1 Meaning of the Word

In everyday language, forgiveness is equated with "apology" and "indulgence", but the actual meaning of the word goes back much further: According to the classic German dictionary the word "forgiveness" goes back to the root of "failure" or "to strike off". In addition, there are word-historical connections to "to give up" or "to renounce". From the thirteenth century onwards, there is a shift in the meaning of the word away from a universal weighting towards a specific understanding. Forgiveness now means "to renounce reparation" or "to excuse". Forgiveness, thus, assumes that a mistake has previously been made or that an error has occurred. An action or comment or opinion was "wrong" or "unusual".

Colloquially, the notion of "forgiveness" implies…

(a) the request for an apology by the one who has acted wrongly, and.
(b) the indulgence and abandonment, the forgetting, and ultimately the "deletion" by the sufferer of this error.

Sociologist Joachim Fischer writes: "The human monopoly of the ability to point thus also makes it possible to point at each other, to point at the other. In the case of conflict, in the case of an injustice experienced by the first subject, a slight, an injury by another subject, this pointing can turn into a 'denunciation', into an 'accusing' (another word for pointing), into an accusation. In the wake of this pointing and denouncing, there can always be the act of avenging, when the first subject (the 'victim') directly inflicts comparable harm on the accused other subject (the 'perpetrator'), *or*—the significant alternative—the act of punishing, when the first subject points to the accused, denounced subject as the 'perpetrator' in *front of third parties* and indirectly claims from them, the summoned third parties, the act of punishing the accused" (Fischer 2018, p. 45).

3.2 The Pace

The temporal aspect is relevant for the assessment of the essence of "forgiveness". Pre- and post-reflection on an issue itself costs time and changes the focus of consideration; after all, the focus of consideration is not on restoring a balance of guilt but on reflecting on the causes of a mistake. Forgiveness looks away from prolonging a subjective experience and intuitive feeling. Forgiveness creates a state of being that allows for communication about the facts themselves by relinquishing a perceived entitlement. The cause of forgiveness is at the center of the argument, not the issue of making amends. This presupposes that the forgiving event is deliberately postponed or even deliberately forgotten. Georg Simmel already drew attention to the importance of the "tempo of reconciliation" in his writing on the quarrel, emphasizing "that the tempo of reconciliation, of forgiving and forgetting, is of great importance for the structural further development of the relationship, that those terminations of the quarrel do not abolish it unless its latent energies have previously found some actualization: Only in the more open or at least more conscious state are they really penetrated by the reconciliatory tendency. Just as one must not learn too quickly if what is learned is to remain with us, so one must not forget too quickly if forgetting is to fully unfold its sociological significance" (Simmel 1968, p. 253). Forgiveness creates mental space, a mental void that overlooks what has happened, if and only if there is time for reflection and reappraisal.

3.3 The Constellation

Forgiveness itself must be asked by the one who has acted unjustly. The one asking for forgiveness asks. The hope that "time will heal all wounds" may not apply to all forms of social interaction. In most cases, what is happening must be actively addressed. This first requires a realization and acknowledgment, i.e. an admission of the "wrong" action. In most cases, a certain context of expectations has been irritated or not fulfilled—a state of affairs that is represented by the idea of a "bad conscience" and presupposes an "inner voice", a supra-personal compass, and thus an anchored moral conception.

To forgive, something must have happened. A return is no longer possible because of the mistake made, the irritating action has been carried out and is therefore real. Only then does an active and personal interaction with the injured party follow—the mere discussion of the facts may contain the chance of healing or the possibility of regaining trust. As a result, the person asking for forgiveness enters into an ambiguous situation. Whether forgiveness will occur is open and involves the risk of rejection and even the exacerbation or unresolved finalization of the conflict. Should forgiveness occur, however, the result is the possibility of a decided forgetting with a view to the future of the time "as it was before".

Forgiveness without antecedents does not make sense: Forgiveness explicitly refers to individual customs, contents of trust, or collectively learned mores that were no longer observed. A person has acted in a way that was not actually "expected of him". An expectation, however, is based on something that has evolved over time, creating promise reliability. Forgiveness is based on the notion of a relational contingency, history of interaction, and (cherished) habits.

3.4 The Gift

It is obvious that, according to the current understanding of the language, the concept of forgiveness, as opposed to pardon, has a broadly religious link. "Forgiveness" emphasizes the function of voluntary "giving," which can never be predicted. It is equally unpredictable: It is never certain whether people will (or can) forgive others. Even an attempt can be aborted. In this sense, it also becomes understandable why Georg Simmel struggled with an explanation of this unplannable social act of forgiving. Forgiveness eludes a learned, logical, and largely perspective-clear context that characterizes modernity, and instead operates in an irrational-seeming context that cannot be fully inferred. Forgiveness, accordingly, is something almost archaically unpredictable and unusual in a clearly structured world of learned sequences of effects. This is not automatically unfavorable or bad. Rather, it shows that forgiveness does not conform to the widespread logic of predictability. The "science of forgiveness" results from the constructive will to connect—thus it is at the same time a healing gift, of the one who forgives and the one who asks for forgiveness.

3.5 Trust

Forgiveness is necessary when the reasons for the underlying trust have not been confirmed but irritated or dissolved. Trust as a social category is a promise of action that is able to provide security and orientation in an unclear world. Trust arises and solidifies as soon as people encounter the familiar.

Word-historically, the term trust goes back to "faithful" and implies the idea that an agent is faithful to the assumed expectations, i.e. his actions will not be unexpected or surprising to previous experiences. The bon mot "Faithful is one who remains faithful to oneself" makes this idea handy.

In the context of systems theory, trust is a function that assigns certain expectations to an actor. As a result, the recipient has clear performance predictions. The actor himself notices that his expectable actions condition feedback reliability and orients his actions according to precisely these anchored prospects. The founder of systems theory Niklas Luhmann clarifies this in the statement: "Trust reflects contingency [...]" (Luhmann 2000, p. 29). This is because two actors act within a clear field of content in certain patterns. In this way, the exchange of information is profoundly effective, even though it is hidden and unsaid—one "trusts each other blindly".

There is no doubt that modern life, in particular, is based on these subliminal, unconscious, and covert information networks. The more complex social circles are, the more we are dependent on fixed points of trust: It is almost no longer possible to deal in a well-founded way with everything and everyone who receives our trust. Luhmann describes this as follows: "Trust is exaggerated information, i.e. it is based on the fact that the person trusting already knows his way around in certain basic respects, is already informed, even if not densely enough, not completely, not reliably" (Luhmann 2000, p. 40).

What is the consequence of such a social expectation structure? By providing information in advance, the degree of complexity of the environment is drastically reduced. The infinite variety of what is theoretically possible becomes manageable through a narrowing of content. This reduction makes rapid communication, action, and decision-making possible and stabilizes the interaction of all actors. The infinity of information and possibilities no longer has to be taken in, processed, and evaluated as a whole but "trust labels" are assigned in a field relevant to the individual, which minimizes the selection effort. This "covering" with information and references provides guiding values for coordinating action and making planned decisions.

Assuming this, the structural dependence of trust and forgiveness becomes clear: Both categories are dependent on each other as psychological dispositions that build on each other. Forgiveness only makes sense if there was previously trust, which was irritated or completely annulled by a certain circumstance or event. Forgiveness implies the idea that the assumed and granted routines were not adhered to by the affected action takers. The saying, "I would not have expected this" clarifies the content directed towards the future. If there is no expectation, then there is no possibility of being "disappointed" and the apology is context-free—unless social customs, in general, have been violated.

The concept of disappointment makes it clear that forgiveness always starts from a "deception". A person does not act truthfully or "as usual" but pretends to do so. Forgiveness, then, presupposes the acting, the deciding person. Forgiveness for the unwanted, unintended makes no sense.

Disappointment is based, on the one hand, on decidedly personal expectations and, on the other hand, on superpersonal, i.e. moral, assumptions regarding cultural rules and prohibitions. For example, it is expected that one will not be cheated on a purchase or threatened on the street for no reason. In a family, people do not lie to each other—they trust each other as a community of fate. These moral fixed points also set trust orientations which—if not adhered to—could be criminally sanctioned and punished (adultery is not a criminal offense). Both forms of expectation, the personal as well as the social, are results of proven or attributed experiences—i.e. concrete contents of action. Forgiveness without trust is void of content. Trust without history is void.

3.6 The Injustice

In the academic discourse on forgiveness, the importance of trust is not yet sufficiently considered. The focus is on the perception of "wrong". However, "being wrong" is not a context-free attribution. Injustice itself is a mostly collectively anchored normative category of "this-is-right" and "this-is-wrong"—especially in a communally moral context. The isolated consideration of "injustice" falls short and fails to recognize the diversity of the sense of injustice. It is much more a matter of the determinant of the affirmation of trust:

Does the other act as I expected him to act—both within social categories and as a personal assessment? Or does the action correspond to an individual but the profoundly collective idea of how it should "actually" be and ultimately not be redeemed? If, for example, a friend cheats me out of money, then this behavior deeply shakes my expectations because here the logic of exploitation of the purposive world suddenly appears in a normally purposeless context.

Forgiveness only works insofar as it is clear what should be respected. Forgiveness, as a social context, is in principle only possible because there is a latent sense that the world, in its myriad interactions, is unpredictable. Trust wants predictability in the form of psychological and social grammar. Predictability as a social mechanism is novel and fragile against the backdrop of human cultural history. However, predictability is all the more important in a world of complexity and acceleration. Thus, it may well be permissible to think that forgiveness is possible because the stability of social-relational actions is diffusely conscious as a special case and—precisely because of the increasing unpredictability of the world—is to be reproduced all the more vehemently and surely.

3.7 The Unplannability

This becomes particularly clear when forgiveness is considered in its phases of action: The philosopher Svenja Flaßpöhler has defined what she sees as the three action areas of forgiveness. Forgiveness presupposes that.

(a) a person recognizes a wrong action,
(b) indicates that, and.
(c) finally refrains from doing so (cf. Dimbath 2018, p. 59).

In this triad, what Simmel called the "enigmatic" mechanism of social interaction occurs: No one has to forgive another person; forgiveness itself is always an individual decision. There is no right to forgive. Forgiveness falls into a category of action that, according to Flaßpöhler, is close to giving—it is not for nothing that we speak of "giving trust" (cited in Dimbath 2018, p. 60).

Whether forgiveness is made possible is not predictable. Now, it becomes clear why Georg Simmel characterizes forgiveness as follows: "There is something rationally incomprehensible in forgiveness, if one seeks to carry it through to the last reason" (Simmel 1992, p. 377).

3.8 And: A Theological Perspective

From a theological perspective, forgiveness is possible because man is a being who can also make mistakes due to his will to make a free decision. Because mistakes characterize man in his myth of existence from the beginning (Genesis "The apple from the tree of knowledge"), this fundamental human experience leads to recognizing mistakes as mistakes and finally even to correct them. For just as man is capable of good, so he is also characterized by the possibility of destructive action.

The understanding of forgiveness as a gift, as a possibility of autonomous context reversal, is a culturally formative fact that is a core content of the Christian faith experience. Thus, the religious celebrations of the Easter Vigil include the following call: Felix culpa (Happy guilt)! The thought behind it: It is only through the annulment of guilt (Jesus's crucifixion) that God has turned his connection to humanity into absolute love. Guilt and forgiveness are "divine" aspects of being human.

This correction breaks the vicious circle of retaliation and puts in its place the solidary empathy in the defectiveness of the human being as such, the communally entangled sensation of the human in the whole range of possibilities.

Forgiveness gives the possibility to become "good", in religious terms, to participate as a witness in divine grace: Not only the one who forgives but also the one who is forgiven receives the possibility to orientate his future actions against the background of the experienced "goodness". Conversion and change are possible and make a man an eternal agent. Man is not a slave to decisions and ways once made but can (and may) go back. Man's life is controllable and implies the possibility of "turning back" until the end. A conception of salvation that, psychologically, implies the eternal possibility of relief: Hardly anything works more deeply.

3.9 Summary: What Characterizes Forgiveness

With recourse to the multi-layered ideas of a "dynamic of forgiveness", different premises emerge which allow the dimensions and stages, for all their variability and mutability, to be traced back to recurring patterns.

The elaborated mosaic stones of a theory of forgiveness can be an orientation to summarize this active, giving, and yet enigmatic action in rough condensation.

- Forgiveness is the failure to consider and/or withdraw a claim.
- The claim results from existing expectations and collectively anchored, i.e. historically learned, notions of a

"right" or "wrong"—thus forgiveness is not universal, but context-bound and anchored in time.
- Forgiveness goes back to an irritated or broken relationship of trust: A person does not act as it is actually expected.
- Forgiveness is a voluntary act. There is no right to forgive.
- Forgiveness is a gift that acknowledges the flawed nature of everything human.
- Forgiveness requires time to test the truthfulness of the apology. Forgiveness requires reflection on the part of the guilty one and the victim. The goal is the successive fading or planned to forget of the offending cause.
- Forgiveness requires an active request, an act of forgiveness. The one asking for forgiveness must acknowledge a faulty behavior.
- As a result, the forgiver and the forgiveness seeker meet on a level that allows for affirmative, supportive communication once again. The breach of trust is revisited in favor of a positive reliability prognosis based on the past.

With these individual-psychological interim results in mind, the following considerations are intended to shed more light on and understand the collective dynamics of forgiveness. How do groups "forgive" their members if they have acted "wrongly"? What does "collective forgiveness" presuppose? What gradations of forgiveness exist and how does the overarching communication of displeasure proceed? How does the "guilty" person become part of the community again? Can identical premises and phases of action be discerned here as well, and how does the interaction proceed between a diffuse group and an individual actor who does not experience his "forgiveness" in person. This requires looking at the ideal types of social alliances and deriving insights for collective forgiveness.

Literature

Dimbath O (2018) Verzeihen, Versöhnen, Vergessen in filmischer Interaktion. In: Morikawa T (ed) Verzeihen – Versöhnen – Vergessen. Transkript, Bielefeld, Germany

Fischer J (2018) Das Verzeihen. Seine Sozialontologie im Lichte der Theorien 'sozialer Akte' und 'Sprechakte'. In: Morikawa T (ed) Verzeihen – Versöhnen – Vergessen. Transkript, Bielefeld, Germany

Luhmann N (2000) Vertrauen. Ein Mechanismus der Reduktion sozialer Komplexität. UTB, Stuttgart, Germany

Simmel G (1968) Der Streit. In: Simmel G (ed) Soziologie. Untersuchungen über die Formen der Vergesellschaftung. Duncker & Humblot, Berlin, Germany

Simmel G (1992) Untersuchungen über die Formen der Vergesellschaftung. Soziologie. Suhrkamp, Frankfurt, Germany

4

About the Collective Will

The public sphere is the result of social relationships between individuals, of groups, and between groups. As more or less different actors, Harald they interact with each other and influence each other in their exchange on a certain topic. Colloquially, "social" is often equated with positive, unifying qualities. Social is what is friendly. In front of a scientific focus, the social is not per se something good or "people-friendly" but first describes forms of social processes.

Now, that it has become clear what forgiveness means and what psychological mechanisms are at work, it is important to better understand the overarching, socially conditioned embeddings. Why? Only in the interplay between I and we do what we understand as the reality of life emerges. Only in this way does it become clear why it is not always only we as a person who decides but above all, we in us decides. Perhaps we forgive differently when we face a person directly than when we are the governors of a collective opinion?

4.1 The Will of the Many: Forms of Social Alliances

As was made clear earlier, the social is subject to a fundamental condition: It must be willed. It arises from the common promotion of an idea, a purpose, an aim.

From the wills of the individuals, a superordinate, common context of wills emerges, a social subject or, in other words, a hyperorganism. The dynamics, forces of attraction, and repulsion of these idea-organisms form the actual objects of an epistemological occupation of social-psychological and sociological systems. Their meaning lies in their purpose-oriented condensation: "For every whole is purpose for itself: this is only another expression for its unity, that is, for its existence as a permanent one, as which is maintained by its own power from moment to moment, though at the same time by concurring favorable conditions, i.e. other, promoting forces" (Tönnies 1991, p. 148).

This social will occurs in two ideal-typical forms: Community and society. There is, as a rule, in each person an intuitive diffuse knowledge of what characterizes these two social forms. Take the trouble and think for a moment about what distinguishes a community from a society …

Very roughly: Communities seem small-scale, more comprehensive, and more profound than society groups, which appear more rational, goal-oriented, and situational in their presence. Communities are close, societies the wide world. We know the family community but not the family society.

So before we can move on to an analysis of public opinion, we will take a closer look at these two forms of alliance.

4.2 The Community

Communities are collectives that have grown through a shared history. For this reason, they appear extremely stable—they are the results of certain habits: Customs and habits of communities change only gradually because they fundamentally shape a person's self-image and sense of place: As a member of a family, a city, an era, a milieu. Their abrupt change would unsettle and disorient the person at his or her core. The community is characterized by a common and concordant will and harmonized assessments. This gives rise to habits and a sense of duty towards others within the community.

According to Tönnies, these quasi-organic communities develop into the "community of spirit" or "community of place". Consequently, communities are always in relation to their environment. The contents of a community are conditioned by factors that are only partly subject to the influence of the people who form them. As the bearers of different communities experience the same things, the forms of communities become similar, forming overlapping social bodies with similar memory. Tönnies clarifies: "Imperceptibly, the habitual passes over into the instinctive, the libidinal: what we are accustomed to do, we do involuntarily [...]" (Tönnies 1909, p. 9). The experiences experienced in communities condense into collective experiences and are cultivated and inherited collectively.

Communities shape our understanding of right and wrong, of wanted and unwanted, and unconsciously condition our preferences. They predefine our sensibilities well before individual deliberation and thought. The habits of culture take possession of us, so that separation between self-will and cultural will, according to Tönnies, hardly seems possible. As Germans, Italians, or Chinese or Indians, we radiate these habits outwards in the way we greet, eat or celebrate Christmas and are immediately recognizable as belonging or different.

Communities are biographically shaped: Man is born into them and they permanently shape behavior and understanding in the world. In a community, an original, natural state is at work, a "unity of will" and feeling resulting from the similar circumstances of life. In it not only the people of the present time work together but also those who sometimes no longer live at all. A heritage of behaviors, speeches, and activities continues to condition actions to this day: From the way, one greets, cooks, celebrates, or when one thinks about choosing a tie to go with a suit. Even if one does not share or reject these choices, these coordinates shape our ideas, values, and feelings. Communities are also always collective places of memory. A community of people bound together in this way marks a bond that largely defies rational decision-making: The promise of marriage, for example, implies standing by each other even if life circumstances should develop for the worse and separation would be perfectly rational for one of the partners. Communal ties are based on emotional commitment and obligation.

Communities are the original forms of living together. Their interactions are usually not documented in writing but they follow a lived culture. The basis for acting within a community is trust; the pattern of action usually functions non-verbally and without a factual resolution.

In communities, there is a natural bond that can hardly be destroyed even by spatial separation or differing views in sub-areas ("A family sticks together."). The common socialization and a fund of a shared destiny maintain the connection over time.

The community, thus, tends to be a form of alliance shaped by the past, whose colorations and traces guide and determine decisions. The French philosopher Francois

Jullien points out: "Nevertheless, as Nietzsche already emphasized, it is true that culture always emerges and develops in a particular territory, in a particular milieu. It always happens locally, in the vicinity, and in a landscape: in a language and in an atmosphere that constitute its conciseness. Even more appropriate than local seems to me the term focal: culture always unfolds from something like a 'hearth' (foyer), through the singular—because only the singular is creative" (Jullien 2018, pp. 53–54).

The communal form of sociality is a familiar expression of social will. Due to their originality and their deeply rooted density, Alexander Deichsel characterizes communities in the following reflection: "They created those social bodies that allowed to survive and to reproduce—as tribe or gender, as peoples or family" (Deichsel 2006, p. 65).

Belonging to a collective enables the individual to form a secure bond with other group members. Conflicts and tensions are reduced based on the same attitudes. By acting as one, communities can achieve group goals more consistently. Estel, therefore, clarifies: "[…] the identity of a collective is gained and preserved less by a negative, so to speak passive demarcation from the outside than by a constantly new realization of collective values and standards or the formation and pursuit (also!) of specific goals oriented towards them in and towards the outside world" (Estel 1983, p. 180).

4.3　The Society

Tönnies writes in his introductory thoughts on society: "The theory of society constructs a circle of people who, as in community, live and dwell peacefully side by side, but are not essentially connected, but essentially separated […]. In so far as here each is alone and in a state of tension against all the rest. […] No one will do and perform anything for the other, no one will want to grant and give anything to the other unless it is for the sake of a counter-performance or counter-gift, which he considers at least equal to what he has given" (Tönnies 1991, p. 34).

A social alliance is constituted by the individual himself. The individual is the initiator, the autonomous will defines the actions. Societies, as social creations, go back to founding personalities who purposefully organize their ideas: As an association, a company, an association of interests. Within this collective, there are clear rules in the form of a fixed agreement, a law, or a contract.

A social group comes together because its members pursue identical goals. They choose each other and interact against the background of the achievement of goals.

In communities, man is, in societies man comes. This makes clear the driving force and the actual distinguishing feature of society with regard to the community: Societies are chosen with a purpose in mind, while communities have their goal in themselves, form it autonomously. In social forms of alliance, each individual wants to optimally assert and maintain his goals vis-à-vis others. An employment contract, for example, regulates salary and working hours—to the advantage of both signatories. In contrast to the community, which is effective for life (even if one willingly breaks away from it), society is limited in its duration due to its purpose character. A society dissolves when a purpose has been achieved.

Tönnies makes this clear in the following quotation: "The theory of society constructs a circle of people who, as in the community, live and dwell side by side in a peaceful way, but are not essentially connected, but essentially separated, and while there they remain connected despite all separations, here they remain separated despite all connectedness" (Tönnies 1991, p. 40). Tönnies identifies economic interactions as the most advanced phenomenon of this form of sociality: Contracts regulate the fulfillment and calculability of interests of exchange and thus of purpose. For this reason, modern sociality has established rules in the form of laws, because with their help social interactions are steered into organized and calculable paths.

Social relations are autonomous and self-determined, they are a consequence of our desires and self-chosen markers. They are based on the decisions and arrangements that the person chooses for himself (as far as he is able)—they are relationships of choice. They make us free because their contents lie within us as almost infinite possibilities. Whoever grew up in a village knows that one always remains "the child of family x". Defined by year and day with this origin. When the big day comes and you leave your village, perhaps to study in the city or to start an apprenticeship, your hand is blank: No one knows you—you are not only free in your own choices, but at the same time in how you are perceived by others.

4.4 The Social Will … in Change

Both forms of will presented do not occur in the reality of life in an extreme either-or. Rather, life as an infinitely interconnected network of interactions always takes place in mixed forms. In this real presence, however, one of the two ideal types predominates, revealing a community or a social will. In all actions, aspects of both ideal types may be present, complementing each other, reinforcing decisions, or always awakening a critical spirit by engaging ourselves as part of a community with the experiences of "our people." It is this oscillation between these forms that leads to progress and the ability to conserve, rethink, and in some circumstances interpret "the existing" in a self-similar, that is, contemporary but typical manner. No community repeats itself exclusively identically—communities too, to survive as cultural systems, adapt to the circumstances of the world but conserve their fundamental success patterns and contents.

And yet postmodern service societies are increasingly shedding their communal dispositions in favor of a borderless hyper culture under the guiding principle of interlocking economic exchange. This tendency can be observed worldwide, even if the westernized systems are stringently leading the way.

The world of late modernity, which moves in small, self-referential units, i.e. communities, contradicts the logic of a growth-oriented order. Instead, the postulate of scaling applies, which wants to make every invention, every product, every service from a smartphone to a restaurant chain or a feature film globally exploitable. The whole world is the market and the internet empowers even the smallest tailor to assume a customer base of potentially 7.5 billion people. The hyperconsumerism of postmodernism only works because all stages of value creation are subject to radical specialization. Products can survive in competitive cut-throat markets because components and work processes are broken down into countless individual steps involving the most cost-effective supplier or service provider in each case. Hardly any products come from a single source—everything disintegrates into a system of rational logic. Only for this reason is it understandable why "old things" that still come from a workshop, from a business, are considered by a master craftsman to be "vintage pieces" that trigger fascination and appreciation. Their value lies in the idea of the "unique piece", the special, the authentic.

At the same time, there is a structural conflict of goals within late modernity: At the moment of the collective discovery of the special, it successively becomes a fashion, a style, i.e. a serial ideal image. What develops out of the multitude of possibilities as a resonant standard giver for something special from the infinity of the market is subject to a high degree of uncertainty in a digitalized communication environment. Which product or service fulfills this momentum, especially with the help of digital channels, often eludes predictable probability at the beginning.

While classical industrial society standardized style patterns in the sense of mass products and disseminated them through advertising, the art of late modernity lies in circumventing this standardization in favor of an aura of the special, and in achieving a perceptible specificity through scarcity while simultaneously gaining collective knowledge about the product. After all, the special is only special if everyone understands that it is special. The desire for specialness becomes a victim of the hunt for social recognition.

The sociologist Andreas Reckwitz describes the effects vividly: "Often the collective style is represented by a brand. The creation of cultural brands, each with its own particular profile, must be understood as a particularly powerful form of late-modern singularization. The design of a brand such as Apple, Hugo Boss or Ligne Roset includes not only the design of the aesthetic style of the consumable objects, but also that of the flagship stores, the advertising presence or the form of the customer approach. The respective brand then stands for its own narrative-sensual world or identity of considerable complexity, in which the consumer participates via iPad, suit or sofa" (Reckwitz 2018, p. 130).

Even the focus on a "green world society" does not eliminate the conflict of goals described above. An economy based on ecological-social premises is already taking place at the margins. The economic stimulus measures and incentives pushed by the state are a remarkable indication that economic actors are guided exclusively by economic factors, however, green their intentions may appear to be. That is, the classical economic notion of growth continues to guide economies. Looking at the formerly local and now globally devastating, home-less digital and platform economic models from Amazon to Google to Airbnb, it is clear that networks based on local customs are steadily in retreat. If one follows the idea that the economy as an overarching sphere, superstructure, or "second nature" (Karl Marx), conditions the fates and developments of social togetherness, the result is an increasing dynamic that cannot be stopped even by insistent appeals to the value of community, and which brings social motives and logics to the fore. For a long time now, it has not only been about the standardization of the global economy but also about life concepts that are becoming generalized and in which the human being as a communal individual has to assert the smallest territories—up to and including the family (e.g. outsourcing of education, absolute mobility, constant accessibility).

This process only succeeds because individuality takes place in serial format. The result is a state in which the individual reduces himself in the illusion of absolute freedom and interchangeability. Individualized television programs and personal shopping recommendations in real-time on the smartphone, personalized children's storybooks are the individualized smoke screens of modernity. Everyone decides freely on their career, their place of residence, their choice of products, their religion, their political preferences, their gender. We mean, think, and act freely with the only problem that the content is profoundly the same and acts as an imperative for the entire world - without feeling like it. As philosopher Richard Schubert clarifies, "Everyone may now dance in Madonna's scuffed feather boa, everyone may write feuilleton without a line fee, may walk in the permanent carnival parade of monadic democracy as a model, blogger, literary critic, himself. Because that no longer has any value anyway. Behind the virtual carnival of self-empowerment, real disenfranchisement is taking place" (Schuberth 2018, p. 131).

The fabrication of the exaltation and defense of individualism in a culture of substantive equality of all acts as a ground noise across all aspects of society. The social is evolving at breathtaking speed from a world of communities to a system in which different societies meet and interact with each other—goal and purpose-oriented.

Ferdinand Tönnies seemed to have anticipated this development as early as the last year of the nineteenth century. In a letter on May 14, 1899, to the Danish philosopher Harald Höffding it can be read: "As far as I know, however, I have never wavered in the judgment that the whole of modern development is essentially negative and critical, precisely because of the prevailing social character which necessarily sustains it; we know clearly that we are past the prime of life and are on the descending branch… I mean that we have to prepare the ground for a new culture which will perhaps only begin its real-life after four to five hundred years, and we can prepare no better ground for it than by instilling into the present old culture as much health and sprightliness as possible. But this is not done by preserving the thoroughly revolutionary, demoralizing and deintellectualizing capitalism and society, nor [by] preserving communities that have become inwardly untrue, such as the church, the monarchy, etc." (Correspondence Tönnies—Bickel and Fechner 1989, p. 65).

In the dominant expediency of social systems, people only superficially come to rest and contemplation to become aware of their deepest point of individuation and confuse the personalized yoga course on the Algarve, the mindfulness seminar via the app, or a conscious diet with a self-moving impulse. All simultaneously harass and affirm each other multiply and fail endlessly because there will always be someone who has "an even more awesome career," "an even more harmonious family," or an even "nicer 1914 family home with real stucco and a view of an undevelopable farmland"-at least in the imagination (see Errichiello 2019).

Perhaps we have never been so little ourselves as we are today—precisely because things seem different, precisely because the logic of this time is not linked to specific actors but all victims are at the same time perpetrators.

With this view of late modernity and with reference to a theory of the social that distinguishes sharply between communal and social ideal types, an attempt can be made to clarify premises regarding a "will of the many".

4.5 Summary: What Characterizes the Collective Will?

- The social arises at the moment when people interact with people, people with things, or people with ideas in an affirmative, beneficial interaction.
- As hyper- or idea-organisms, the social will appears as a quasi-person.
- Hyperorganisms are as "real" to perception and judgment as people or groups.
- The social will can be separated into two ideal types. The communal will is historically based and is a form of the intuitive will of the heart. The social will is autonomous, purposeful, situational, and directed towards the future.
- Late modernity has not abolished or weakened the need for social ties but merely changed the forms of connection.
- In a world of hyper-complexity and rapid acceleration, socially-oriented organizations are increasingly taking the place formerly occupied by communal alliance systems.

- Social interactions and connections are characterized by their purposefulness. For this reason, they are more variable and volatile—they are subject to a time-bound exchange mechanism.
- For the person of late modernity, the price of high individualization options is the loose rooting of oneself—all areas of life are subject to exchange against the background of constant optimization of adaptation.

Literature

Bickel C, Fechner R (1989) Briefwechsel Ferdinand Tönnies – Harald Höffding, Beiträge zur Sozialforschung (BSO), Bd, vol 4. Duncker und Humblot, Berlin

Deichsel A (2006) Markensoziologie. Deutscher Fachverlag, Frankfurt, Germany

Errichiello O (2019) Einsamkeit und die Kraft der Marke. Springer, Wiesbaden, Germany

Estel B (1983) Soziale Vorurteile und soziale Urteile. VS Verlag, Opladen, Kritik und wissenssoziologische Grundlegung der Vorurteilsforschung

Jullien F (2018) Es gibt keine kulturelle Identität. Suhrkamp, Berlin

Reckwitz A (2018) Die Gesellschaft der Singularitäten. Suhrkamp, Berlin

Schuberth R (2018) Narzissmus und Konformität. Selbstliebe als Illusion und Befreiung. Matthes & Seitz, Berlin

Tönnies F (1909) Die Sitte. Rütten und Loening, Frankfurt, Germany

Tönnies F (1991) Gemeinschaft und Gesellschaft. Grundbegriffe der Reinen Soziologie, Wissenschaftliche Buchgesellschaft, Darmstadt, Germany

5

About Opinions of Many

Communities and societies communicate their givens and proscriptions, their communicative resonant spaces, in different forms of opinion. In order to understand collective forgiveness, it makes sense to familiarize oneself with a socio-psychological understanding of public opinion. It helps to penetrate reality more clearly in the thicket of the everyday intermingling of opinion, information, and news. And above all, to understand collective forgiveness, it is crucial to understand how a supra-personal judgment is formed in the first place.

5.1 Public and Public Opinion

The Internet and the relevant business networks seem like heavenly pastures of salvation: Wonderful visions, scenarios, and concepts for the future are sprouting everywhere. Futurologists and trend researchers are enigmatically and luridly catering to the desire for a tangibly better world. Media makers are happy to take up the pallid outlook and diligently spread the agenda: Ecology, fairness, and solidarity. The message is it is just around the corner—soon, very soon, we will create a better, eco-fair world. The solidarity of the human race is just a stone's throw away—the many shopping aids, neighborhood initiatives, flash mobs, editorials written with verve and posh gossip happenings in times of crisis are just a taste of truly revolutionary conditions. And the whole world of journalists and creatives follows suit—quite serially-individually—with an inexhaustible staccato of emphatic commentaries, "white papers" and "thought pieces" on post-capitalist society. Everyone gets to fantasize and, quite incidentally, powerfully blog away their irrelevance in an age of nearly 8 billion people while taking a global stand. People make their relevance clear to each other by vigorously pressing all the "like" buttons worldwide. Echo chambers of the global intelligentsia. So it is, though the results of our actions might as well not be: The world would not be different …

Public opinion is an individual, concrete creature of ideas that are not tangible in the sense of clear physical boundaries, that no human being has ever met in its entirety but which, as a subject of perception, (co-)determines people's actions and guides their power of judgment. Tesla, Germany, Hamburg, or "the state" are ideal realities—even if they are much more than a tangible product, a building, or a constitution. People talk about all the listed forms, give their opinion, their judgment, and sometimes enter into a conflict of views and judgments. Hyperorganisms are mosaic stones of the self-image and the subjective perceptions associated with them, which make us followers, opponents, or indeterminate-uninvolved users or observers. By telling about "our things", our favorite restaurant, our preferred vacation spot, our favorite book, we are also always telling about ourselves and how we want to be seen (incidentally, this presupposes an equal notion of content). Crucially, these levels of judgment can be differentiated against an analytical background. Analogous to the idea that people form either communal or social alliances, opinions can also be ordered into two ideal types.

5 About Opinions of Many

Public opinion is a result of the civilization, in which more and more communities came together and the ability of a community to assert itself through war or violence required many forces and resources. In contrast, a state of affairs had to be brought about in which two communities organized themselves peacefully with regard to one issue—for example, originally over the use of a watering hole or an area that provided food. This required contracts first discussed orally and later even written down. The contract implies the understanding of understanding in that people agree on their behavior now and in the future. It is clear that public opinion is a product of human compression as an outgrowth of modern times, which over the centuries has produced increasingly diverse and differentiated forms of collective will. It aims to bring people and their communities into an order that ensures their survival and growth as a delimited community—precisely because of its complexity and permanent clash. A paradox arises: To ensure the vitality of communities, socially based relationships with other communities are concluded.

The observance of these contracts is subject to testing and weighing. In the style of his time, Tönnies wrote in "Kritik der Öffentlichen Meinung": "All men capable of thought have and cherish certain 'opinions' about the so-called divine and so-called human things, about processes of nature and of cultural life, past, present, future; more or less definite, more or less firm and decisive 'opinions'. When these views are called 'opinions', this designation contains an indication of their multiplicity and diversity, and therefore also of their subjectivity, and thus of the fact that they often contradict and oppose one another, and to a large extent exclude one another, so that of the opposing ones only one can be 'right', while the other must be 'wrong', unless both are incorrect" (Tönnies 2002, p. 37). Tönnies makes it clear that analogous to the transformation of civilization from community to society, meaning develops from belief to knowledge. The community, he argues, is shaped by given, handed-down opinions, beliefs, and dogmas that are passed down from generation to generation (cf. Tönnies 2002, p. 115).

At first glance, it seems that the world today is not characterized by a single opinion, with clear messages: Every country, every culture, every association, and every person rightly claims to have not just one but its own opinion and to represent it powerfully. Whether these are individual points of view or the reproduction of enforced views is irrelevant in a structural view. What counts is the contemporary self-perception and self-representation as an autonomously deciding and acting individual. Whether this is a real analysis of the depth of individualization in postmodernity or an idealized wishful image as an effective decision-maker is one of the most discussed questions of the present time (see pp. 37–39). Already the social-scientific grandmaster Theodor Adorno let us know,, that it would be a presumption on the part of the vast majority of people to use the word "I".

It is by no means the case that the zeitgeist ideal of individuality actually conceals a firework of diversity. Rather, a closer look at people reveals the devastating and sometimes soul-crushing realization of how alike people of the twenty-first century think and act. The real achievement of late modernity and its manifold actors is much more than the crucial food points, such as education, work and consumption play out and enact a communicative agenda of standardized variant richness. An example of this is the diversity of selectable fields of study, school majors, training, life plans, genders, "tailor-made" products (from the hand-kneaded pizza in the freezer shelf to the fish manufactory), or services (Airbnb or Authentical Experiences on Trip Advisor).

Of the 100 billion or so people who have lived on this planet, very few have been truly groundbreakingly "different" and able to briefly change the course of the world or at least some of its segments. To the point: At its core, it is about building a house by the urban stormwater detention pond, shopping well, controlling your weight to some degree, and (maybe) eventually having kids. We enrich the filling time in between with all sorts of exotic trips first with and then without backpacks, tandem flights, and county league soccer games—well insured, of course … there is nothing honorable about that; on the contrary, it is something extremely reassuring.

And precisely for this reason, the decisive medium for realizing individuality remains one's own opinion. Wherever you look: A concert of conflicting views and opinions. But not only the person appears as an "opinion machine", but the public world is also full of newspapers, TV channels, discussion forums, district conferences, experience exchange meetings, workshops, blogs, and news magazines.

The sociologist Rainer Waßner has sharply elaborated this connection. He writes: "He [Tönnies] finally identifies 'opinion' as an opinion and a holding for what is right for reasons that can be stated, in contrast to unquestioning faith, which 'is whole and uniform devotion to the person or the thing'. […] Accordingly, to believe is actually to believe someone, a relation which is not possible for what is mine … belief is a matter of the heart, what is mine of the head.' Faith one has only one, opinions infinitely many. And of opinions, in turn, he is interested only in publicly expressed and, above all, unifying opinions. Any statement from anywhere and anyone is sociologically irrelevant" (Waßner 2020, p. 5).

The specificity of a coordinate system lies in a social state of affairs, which Tönnies precisely grasps with the term "public opinion". This opinion, which is social for a respective community, is a result of considerations and experiences, which, despite all the differences of the members, presupposes a commonality and agreement of opinions at certain points. This commonality of classification and will ultimately lead to a collective binding force and an overarching context of obligation: This opinion is correct for this association. As a social control authority, public opinion is a perpetual, self-active body that verifies and adheres to the collective will of a group—independent of existing institutions. This collective will emanates from an overarching social will that has the greater whole in view and precisely not the self-interests of countless, hermetically sealed communities.

5.2 Ethics and Morals

This view of the big picture, boldly called ethics, has humanity in mind. Ethics stands in contrast to morality, which comprises the customs, commands, and prohibitions of a community, for example, a family or an association of interests. Morality is local, self-referential, multifaceted, and always in competition with other moralities ("The morality of the troop!"). Ethics tries to establish overarching, purpose-oriented rules—independent of place and time ("The ethics of humanity!").

Accordingly, Tönnies differentiates between two ideal types, analogous to the "social", also in the case of public opinion: Published opinion as the mouthpiece of ethics and public opinion as the channel of action and communication of morality.

Here the following applies: "In truth, public opinion always wants to be an impartial opinion, not determined by interests; it asserts what it advocates as the right thing, the thing dictated by reason, recommended by science, based on the best authorities, or necessary in the sense of the general good, securing a better future" (Tönnies 2002, p. 316).

Public opinion is a kind of "imaginary court of justice" (Ferdinand Tönnies), which treats all people equally—without regard to the person—and calls for overarching action. Regardless of whether it is foreign groups, one's people, or a community gathering. Public opinion protects and secures the understanding of a community. Tönnies states: "Thus understood, public opinion is the common mode of thought, the cooperative spirit of any group or association, insofar as its opinion is based on thought and knowledge, as is first and most easily the case in matters of daily life, common utility, and the common and unifying ideas of a social class [...]" (Tönnies 2002, p. 99).

Crucial to public opinion is its unanimity about all phenomena and facts that we as humans perceive: The actions of other people, communities, nations, associations, or even religious communities, to name a few.

As a political-philosophical concept, the dream of human unity is closely interwoven with the European Enlightenment of the eighteenth century. In Friedrich Schiller, this spirit is vividly echoed when he describes the task of the theatre: "Each individual enjoys the raptures of all [...] and his chest now gives way to only one sensation—it is this: to be one human being" (quoted in Wertheimer 2020, p. 338). And in Beethoven's "Ode an die Freude" ("Ode to Joy") the decisive line of the song is "All men become brothers"—not surprisingly, the lyricist here was also Friedrich Schiller.

Public opinion itself differentiates—in a scientific context—into different levels of density, duration, and thus impact solid, liquid, and volatile (cf. Tönnies 2002). This categorization, abstract at first glance, makes practical sense, especially when evaluating collective forgiveness because each of these aggregate levels has implications for the culture of forgiveness. The three levels are:

5.3 The Firm Public Opinion

"*Firm* Public Opinion is a general, unshakable belief of the public representing [...] a whole people or a wider circle of 'civilized humanity'" (Tonnies 2002, p. 165).

This describes human rights and fundamental values, such as human dignity and freedom, which stand above all cultural anchors or laws. These principles are overarching, non-negotiable, and, as it were, eternally binding.

5.4 The Liquid Public Opinion

Contemporary collective views are formulated that repeatedly fall back on the firm foundations that have been pointed out. Here, it is a question of issues, such as generational justice, equality between women and men, or also—quite specifically—climate protection. Crucially, these issues may well be valued differently by different actors. Also, the contents may be irrelevant or hardly relevant for certain communities, but the "measure of things" for others—at least in a manageable time frame (as a rule, these are so-called macro-trend topics, which have a media relevance period of 3–5 years). The actual manifestations of the presented basic values are therefore objects of the time and culture. They may determine the agenda of politics and society for several years, but their contents may have different variants and characteristics.

5.5 The Fleeting Public Opinion

In his analysis, Rainer Waßner has worked out that the "volatile" public opinion comes to light above all in the published opinions. Television or blog, radio or newspaper, they all work with the announcement of large or small excitements, supposed advantage. Waßner makes their dynamics handy: "In them—this is the main Tönniesian idea—the specifications of solid and fluid public opinion, the merely imagined perspective of *humanity* [sic!] mix with the particular local, situational, temporal circumstances, the personal, commercial and ideological conditions and interests of the publicists to form the profile of a broadcast, a newspaper, a program, a director, an online magazine, etc." (Waßner 2020, p. 5).

From this follows: Public opinion, as an opinion above all else, wants to make itself known publicly, i.e. universally, uniformly as an ethical will, as an expression of an assembly that is never assembled but which, as the spiritual subject of a totality, influences the actions of the people of a common consciousness with—as was made clear above—varying quality of enforcement, sustainability and temporal relevance.

5.6 Public Opinion as the "right voice within us"

Now, the function of public opinion becomes clearer: It is an informal insurance and control system of the general public—quite independent of the diversity and normativity of the communities embedded in it. As a signaling and corrective organ, this "social fact" (Max Weber) judges the actions and deeds of people and groups. Long before an issue can be legally addressed, perhaps never legally addressed, public opinion takes over the judgment by commanding that "you don't do that" or that this is "not okay." Thus, public opinion is a spontaneous, improvised, and transparent court of law with a newsworthy quality. It characterizes a direction and a generalized will that claims to speak for the unassembled All. In doing so, it even questions and unconditionally tests authority. Its assertiveness across cultures and ages is rooted in the insight that, against the backdrop of an increasingly complex or narrow world, an ethical view intuitively safeguards the life chances of any community. The categorical imperative (i.e., firm public opinion) is the life insurance of even the smallest human design variant—whether it concerns the rights of the Catalans, indigenous peoples of Canada, the Frisians on the North Sea coast, or the Sorbs in the Spree forests.

This "intentional order" is to be understood as social order: People or groups sometimes violate the way we have organized our life together. The reliability of togetherness is endangered by lies, untruthfulness, violation of rules, or taking advantage. Openness, comprehensibility, and calculability are not realized in the way that the interaction of two equal partners requires. Beyond trust, the connectivity of the interaction is endangered because the respect and appreciation of the other are not realized. Reliability as a condition of a sociality connected in diverse networks requires expectability and ideal automatisms in order to function smoothly and quickly.

In a late modern society, traditional and modern media act as instances for public opinion. Tönnies himself calls these actors "public opinion"—today we would speak of published opinion. They are the opener, initiator, and companion of a trustworthy adherence to ethical rules. A violation is usually called a "scandal". The Greek term "scandalon" goes back to the word meaning to cause a nuisance.

The judgment of "wrong" (not necessarily wrongful) conduct weighs more heavily than many a court judgment because it is based on hearsay and deepens informal knowledge of an issue. As a "bad reputation," it can mercilessly destroy careers and resumes. As negative prejudice, public opinion reverberates.

5.7 Purpose and Meaning of Prejudice

The role of prejudice as the energy of social systems is immense: In the literal sense, prejudice is a judgment made on the basis of insufficient or one-sided information and generally applied to an object or its variants. Even when further information is received, the judgment once made—despite evidence to the contrary—is not revised or at most weakened. The work of the social psychologist Gordon W. Allport from the 1950s and 1960s is considered a classic of prejudice research. Allport summarized in 1954: "Perhaps the shortest of all definitions of prejudice is: Thinking ill of others without sufficient justification. This terse formulation contains the two essential elements of all relevant definitions: the reference to the unfoundedness of the judgment and to the tone of feeling" (Allport 1971, p. 20). Anitra Karsten defined categorically in 1978: "By a prejudice I mean […] a preconceived and negative judgment about groups of people (or an impersonal entity, an idea, a situation, a behavior), and specifically a judgment that is emotionally underpinned and inconsistent with reality" (Karsten 1978, p. 122). However, Allport already pointed out the ambiguity of prejudice. Allport writes: "It [the above definition] is, however, too short for complete clarity. First of all, this formulation refers to negative prejudice. But some also have positive prejudices about others" (Allport 1971, p. 20).

The understanding of prejudice has changed in recent decades. The more complex and confusing sociality becomes, the more impossible it becomes to make balanced judgments. The modern world functions based on a multitude of focalizations, foreshortenings, reductions in knowledge, and collectively shared half-truths. It seems that from this realization, research no longer places the "truth content" of the term prejudice at the center of definitional efforts. Rainer Erb formulated in the mid-1990s: "From this sociological view of prejudice, it becomes clear what decisive importance is attached to the image of society as the fundamentally binding context of prejudice formation or prejudice criticism" (Erb 1995, p. 17).

Accordingly, prejudices are not explicitly undesirable phenomena; they arise in a social context and have a "social function" (Karsten 1978, p. 6). As an individual psychological construct, they are able to give people manageable decision options—negative as well as positive.

It is all the more difficult when this social function is not fulfilled. This leads to irritations that are capable of weakening the fragile balance of informal networks sooner or later: Societies lose orientation.

5.8 A Governing Body

Public opinion preserves a reality of life that seeks to detect transgressions and violations to preserve established or well-rehearsed processes and contents and to avoid irritations caused by breaches of trust. It acts, as it were, as a controlling radar device and drags transgressions into the light—often revealing the unsaid. In this way, public opinion represents loyalty to one's community: A consensus on content is permanently renewed and reassured by public resonance, by making a transgression public. As a social corrective, it reminds us of the existing ideal. The momentum of the respective public excitement serves as a gauge for the overarching acceptance of informal expectations and a notion of "right and wrong". In this sense, public opinion is permanently self-adjusting—its utility arises from the moment. The overarching resonance is therefore a low-threshold means of self-assurance for a real or even imagined group. As a bundling element, public opinion always needs to be as present as possible; its contents are usually fleeting and difficult to grasp. The benefit arises from the moment. Long-past breaches of trust hurt less, are sometimes even jovially noted with a smirk "about that time". Because in the meantime the framework conditions and the people have changed: "back then I would have been annoyed, today we can laugh about it."

At first glance, public opinion reveals a structural contradiction: On the one hand, public opinion calls for socially ethical action; on the other hand, control and enforcement take place through the informal exclusion or reintegration of a moral community. This constellation of opposites is all the more fascinating because the notion of acting honestly is predisposed across all specific cultures and encompasses more than situational conflict resolution. As a rule, there is more behind a scandal or a violation of rules than the concrete case or occasion—much more decisive is the notion of an all-embracing "right" or "wrong" that happens to manifest itself in an example. Precisely because the unconditional rules of a community still have an ethical superstructure, they are capable of critically questioning themselves and optimizing themselves as clearly delimited systems, and becoming aware of their substantial fixed point.

Equipped with the tool of "public opinion", we now have a new perspective on collective forgiveness: Although both personal forgiveness and collective forgiveness are generally characterized by a break with expectations or prejudices, in the case of collective forgiveness, however, there is also the orientation towards transcultural orientation markers that are valid and enforced over long periods of time about the question of how the world and people should be. The categorical imperative or the "Golden Rule" is also regarded here as a guiding principle—a webmaster of modernity. A constant guardian of virtue (or end boss) in the background. It is important to note, however, that collective forgiveness, in the form in which it is examined here, always assumes that a group forgives an individual. This differentiation is crucial, as it is not about groups forgiving one another. It is true that institutionalized forms of "apology" or "asking for forgiveness" can be found, particularly in political and religious discourse; for example, in 2000, then-Pope John Paul II apologized for the errors and crimes committed in the name of the Catholic faith, and in 2008, Canadian Prime Minister Stephen Harper apologized to Aboriginal peoples for suffering and injustice (the then-Chief of the Assembly of First Nations in Canada thanked him at the time for the "symbolic gesture").[1]

The problem that forgiveness would mean a personal towards and towards, as Hannah Ahrendt pointed out at the time, is then comprehensible insofar as the relation of two groups and their representatives is concerned: Apology and forgiveness can de facto only be of a symbolic nature because the actors do not appear as causers, not even as ambassadors but only as representatives for an organization that has changed structurally or as we have called it a hyperorganism. The culprit himself stands at a distance from his group. The present investigation, however, takes as its starting point a person who is the cause of irritation and who stands in relation to a group in whose field of action he has

---

[1] https://www.welt.de/welt_print/article2097765/Indianer-danken-Kanada-fuer-Bitte-um-Entschuldigung.html

hitherto acted. The group itself may have different degrees of density, may sometimes be diffuse, but it is capable of directly grasping and sanctioning a wrong action (informally, legally, or through published opinion).

Summary: What characterizes public opinion?

- Public opinion is a creature of ideas.
- As a creature of ideas, public opinion structures an ethical worldview in varying degrees of effectiveness.
- Ethics is understood as the global interconnectedness of all human beings.
- Public opinion tracks down and publicizes ethics violations.
- The violation usually lies in the non-fulfillment or irritation of enforced expectations and prejudicial dispositions. Public opinion is based on the observance of normative reliabilities.
- In the publication of an "honest" image of man, a community assures itself of its solidarity and permanently charges the normative ideas of "right and wrong".
- Communities are moralotopes—groups in which conformities, expectations, and regulations apply.
- Morality is understood as a group- or community-based attachment of certain people. Morality is an attitude for one's interest.
- Morality is not ethical.
- The public opinion uses ethical content to ensure the coherence and stability of specific groups and to reinforce the reliability of commitments to action.

Literature

Allport GW (1971) Die Natur des Vorurteils. Kiepenheuer & Witsch, Köln

Erb R (1995) Die Diskriminierung von Minderheiten. Wie entstehen Vorurteile? In: Lengfeld H (ed) Entfesselte Feindbilder. Edition Sigma, Berlin

Karsten A (1978) Vorurteil. Ergebnisse psychologischer und sozialpsychologischer Forschung. Wissenschaftliche Buchgesellschaft, Darmstadt, Germany

Tönnies F (2002) Kritik der öffentlichen Meinung. Walter de Gruyter, Berlin

Waßner R (2020) Die Öffentliche Meinung als Nachfolgerin der Religion. Meinungskämpfe und Meinungsbündnisse in der Moderne. Unveröffentlichter Aufsatz, Hamburg, Germany

Wertheimer J (2020) Europa. Geschichte seiner Kulturen. Pinguin, München, Germany

6

About the Collective Forgiveness

An analytical understanding of collective forgiveness touches on different dimensions: From the autonomy of the individual to the collective will, prejudice, forgiveness as a cultural technique, and public opinion. It also becomes clear that there is a structure to forgiveness and that stages of forgiveness can be delineated—no matter how different the specific backgrounds. But even if one applies the findings of the sciences, the decisive factor for forgiveness remains indeterminable: The emotional decision. All too often we feel whether to trust another person again and bear the consequences on our responsibility. This intuitive decision also applies to collectives, even if the steps and time horizons are different.

The aim is now to develop a kind of outline of thoughts on a theory of collective forgiveness—with all its scientific limitations. After all, the analysis is still largely on the surface, as each of the previously mentioned fields would have required an in-depth, well-founded, and epoch-spanning penetration. However, even if the areas highlighted are not yet listed in-depth, initial insights can be gained into what collective forgiveness means and in what forms, structures, and time horizons it occurs. This is and remains all the more important because the integration of public opinion is causal for forgiveness and does not play a role in the discussion so far.

Ultimately, this theory of collective forgiveness "in progress" tries to be a kind of guideline to check whether the basic conditions for forgiveness are given at all and in which phase of forgiveness the actors are.

So what are the seven stages of collective forgiveness?

6.1 The Collective Forgiveness … Conveys Information

As a standard giver of socially desirable and undesirable behavior, collective forgiveness, as an exploration of perception, probes the limits and content of ethics. It is a communication that is nowhere deposited, nowhere verifiable, and that requires its active and immediate reassurance to nevertheless be effective as a guide. Collective forgiveness needs the transgression, the violation, the breaking of rules, to make intuitive regulations tangible in reality and thus to make learning possible. As a social reference and coordinate system, it is characterized by a notion of the closeness of all people and an overarching kinship of the essence.

6.2 Collective Forgiveness … is a Psychological Mechanism of Liberation

By placing individual transgressions at the center of a public discussion, the burdensome fears of a community become apparent. In extreme cases, the idea that wrong or unsolidary behavior causes the break-up of a community has an effect. In addition to the orientation function, publicizing leads to an initial collective dampening of fear: The collective assures itself of its vigilance and thus initiates the first steps towards securing itself. Fear becomes action and thus a psychologically liberating outlet.

6.3 Collective Forgiveness … Exists Only when there is the Freedom to Choose a Decision

Freedom of choice presupposes that people can make their decision intuitively, on the basis of their aesthetic judgment, or in a forward-looking and deliberative way. Because every human being can err and is fundamentally aware of the experience of a wrong decision, there is the possibility of relativizing an action that was unexpected and wrong. The "everyone makes mistakes" (in theological terms: The original sin of man) can lead to solidarity with a guilty person. In this way, individual guilt is generalized and, as it were, located in a natural way. Not the individual acts, but the human acts in us. This implies general forgiveness.

6.4 Collective Forgiveness … is a Mechanism that Restores Trust in a Relationship Constellation

Forgiveness is necessary when a person has not acted as experience with him would have suggested per se, or as is consistent with culturally embedded customs—the behavior was unreliable. However, this view assumes that objective information exists, a standard of truth, and most importantly, a perception of realities that is identical for all people. This is a delusion. Oswald Spengler has made this vividly clear: "One day the last portrait of Rembrandt and the last bar of Mozart's music will have ceased to be, although a painted canvas and a sheet of music may remain because the last eye and ear that was accessible to their formal language disappeared. Ephemeral is every thought, every belief, every science, as soon as the spirits are extinguished in whose worlds their 'eternal truths' were felt to be true by necessity." (Spengler 1986, p. 217).

It is clear that even the idea of an ethical conditionality of man corresponds to culture, point of view, and zeitgeist. Truth is always a social construct. However, by forgiving, there is the prognosis that the person asking for forgiveness will in the future again act in the way that was previously customary or in accordance with the standards of the offended community. Forgiveness itself seems to be able to suppress a thoroughly negotiable discourse on content in favor of forgiveness itself.

6.5 Collective Forgiveness … is, in Relation to a Collective Level, a Result of Public Opinion

The widespread notion that forgiveness presupposes an intimate interaction between two people proves the reality of life that collectives recognize and punish offenses and usually allow for reinstatement into a community. Public opinion characterizes an improvised system of command and prohibition that is not subject to group-specific standardization but rather places the "greater whole of humanity" as the message at the center of expectation. Collective forgiveness is—according to its basic understanding—always an invitation, a taking possession of the options, which at the same time contributes to social cohesion.

6.6 Collective Forgiveness … Succeeds when the One Who Actively Asks for Forgiveness Publicly Confesses and Addresses his Offending Actions

To whom should someone apologize whose actions have concretely harmed far fewer people than feel affected by them? Thus, receiving special favors as a public figure (for example, a politician who allows himself to be opulently invited to dinner on several occasions) may hardly harm anyone directly, and yet a "wave of indignation" and incomprehension may take effect. The public irritation is so vehement for reasons of equal treatment: When a person receives these perks, it is not only unfair (since everyone else usually has to pay for his meal) but the general idea arises that a person no longer distinguishes between "right and wrong". The concrete fact is generalized.

The real value of collective forgiveness, thus, lies in its stabilizing function for the community. The expectation has been disappointed. There is only a chance of forgiveness when the one asking for forgiveness makes his guilt public, i.e. confesses before all the world his fallibility and situational audacity. This form of humility proves to be a way of reducing one's own, as it were, previously overriding importance and of reconnecting to a core element of public opinion, the equality of all human beings. Confessing personal guilt is the key to acknowledging one's shortcomings as a human being through a "mea culpa" and re-establishing one's faith in reliability.

6.7 Collective Forgiveness … Has an Exemplary, Unique, and Infinite Effect

In contrast to legal punishment, which does not necessarily demand an admission of guilt or insight into wrongdoing after a sentence has been served, an unsaid but always subliminal claim follows the person who has been forgiven: In forgiveness, the power of the sanctioning community and the humility of the individual has an exemplary and indefinite effect. For this reason, a community makes sure of exemplary cases, even long past ones, in order to show perspectives and to illustrate the efficacy of communal activities. Social forgiveness is a sanction that is not controlled by an official power and allows a group to become aware of the hidden resonance and acceptance of its followers. Individuals, shaped by the influence of their social environment and comparison with others, can use their usually righteous behavioral inventory to experience individual enhancement as a result.

Literature

Spengler O (1986) Der Untergang des Abendlandes. Umrisse einer Morphologie der Weltgeschichte. dtv, München, German

7

Final Thoughts on: Why Forgiveness Makes us Human

Why is this book relevant? Because the world has never needed forgiveness as much as it does now. This is not because people are more selfish, self-willed, or evil than they were decades or centuries ago—presentism and cultural scolding are a recurring motif of generational detachment and tend to obscure the view rather than provide a structural analysis of the status quo—but because the supposed evil is rooted in the complexity and interconnectedness of all aspects of everyday life. Diversity causes mistakes. Mistakes lead to injuries. Injuries permeate human relationships.

7.1 Thoughts on Forgiveness in Times of Haltlessness

Late modernity works because it has to work. Its real fuel is pauselessness and the absence of delay: Production chains run "just in time", training and teaching is structured in such a way that their levels and modules interlock via general content and certificates, interactions of all kinds are pervaded by a network of connectivity in language, habitus, and content. Communication is everything and requires a basic understanding of comprehension so that explanations are kept to a minimum—they cost time and involve the possibility of a breakdown in communication. We all basically "understand" "how to treat each other", what is good for children or a relationship, or how to treat the sick and weak. The modern world is based on social action synapses being interlocked and connectable. There does not have to be a lot of talking anymore.

The greatest danger occurs to the functioning of an infinitely complex world when the ability to communicate or cooperate comes into jeopardy: The effective machinery of almost silent functioning could falter—not only in relation to the actual actors but from there into many other areas. In a world limited to small, regional functional units (for example, the village of the Middle Ages), where linkages occur only at the margins of the system, the communal quality of the relationship means that leaving the group is virtually impossible, thereby systemically safeguarding connectivity. In a world that is increasingly socially structured (see pp. 33–36), whose interactivity is purposeful and temporal, communication breakdowns are not only possible but frequent. This risk is limited by the process of collective trust in order, on the one hand, to demonstrate forgiveness as an exemplary individual cultural technique and, on the other hand, to cultivate and anchor the ethics of forgiveness as a conducive mosaic stone of the self-image of a so-called "civilized society" in a communicatively elaborate manner.

Our modern self-image is shaped by the will to be "good": No longer is an abstract, individual "good feeling" the focus of consideration, but the struggle for all that is good in the world is the fuel of late modernity. Humans are the UN in miniature, heralds of the good news, the categorical imperative on the cozy relaxing sofas of this world: Hermetic hyperethics. Everyone is getting in on the act, even and especially corporations: Pepsi doing a Peace campaign (failed before airing), Fritz Cola themed G20, Gilette the new man (failed after airing), Dove the natural look (massive sales drop), Coca Cola sponsoring Christopher Street Days ("Hate can't celebrate."), to list just the biggest players. Italian advertiser Oliviero Toscani's credo, delivered with verve in the late 1980s ("Advertising is a smiling carrion. Stop dumbing down through advertising."), whose Benetton campaign used child labor, environmental pollution, or AIDS as advertising motifs for sweaters (and thus led the Benetton company into crisis ...) has been widely accepted. If you look at the big names of the New Economy, they publicly claim to be the ideal type of a new economic model, nothing less than the improvement of the world. Google founder Larry Page writes of the goals of the Alphabet holding company: "Improving the lives of as many people as we can". So the blueprints of a post-capitalist economic system have long since ceased to come from upright Marxist theorists, but from people like Elon Musk or Mark Zuckerberg ... the world has become a crazy place. In marketing, by the way, they write about the target value "hyper-relevance" in this regard ...

One thing man no longer wants to be: A selfish rascal.

However, the fact that the preconditions for (Western) ethics lie in the merciless displacement, skimming, and scaling in all areas of the world and the life of existing economic, mostly local structures hardly comes to light. On the contrary, the more ruthlessly the global struggle for resources, life chances, and hierarchies is waged, the more the symbolic will for equality serves the purpose of calming real action in favor of a good conscience. Real revolutions, an actual change of the conditions is still not recognizable. Human nature apparently does not change even through ethical appeals. The three C's of children, credit, and car have so far sedated (almost) every barricade hero.

Collective forgiveness is not the result of the increasingly reflective behavior of people with and among each other, but it is a necessity to maintain and safeguard the ability of modern civilizations to function and connect. Safeguarding means two aspects: On the one hand, collective forgiveness as a process of public arousal, discussion, and pacification is one of the last bastions where "communality" in the sense of an overarching will becomes effective. On the other hand, collective forgiveness secures the ability to connect, in that faulty or community-damaging behavior can be taken back and, as it were, healed.

The late-modern world tries to implement equal treatment and freedom of autonomy as a core principle of public and private premises of action as comprehensively as possible: Kindergarten children choose next week's food via smiley for lack of writing skills, adults determine their gender, gender-neutral language avoids a wrong mindset, quotas for women, migration background, marital status are enshrined in law and sometimes even enforced … while the thought behind these developments may be ethically comprehensible, an analytical view recognizes much deeper and structural traits of self-perception. The absolute valorization of individualistic possibilities for development and growth takes hold as the contemporary nature of people in the twenty-first century, when the possibility of a successful, fulfilled life is limited to the earthly lifespan. This thought, which is "quite natural" for us, is, however, more than new and innovative in view of the intellectual history of man. For thousands of years, people believed that earthly life was a stage, a step on the way to their gods, paradises, and purgatories—time on earth was a test for better or worse.

Now, for a large part of the world's population, especially in Western countries, the belief in life after death is generating less and less resonance. As a consequence, the 70 or 80 years on this planet alone and without exception are the measure of all things, the playing field on which a fulfilled life can succeed. The "earthly now" forms the coordinate system for dreams, desires, and actions. This mentality, which is most effective unconsciously, seeks out spaces and objects that stand as synonyms for the achievement of goals: In addition to altruistic attributions such as love, affection, respect, or appreciation, it is purchasable goods and services that make clear to us, but also the environment: I am realizing my dreams and I have made it. The visible grandeur as a Porsche in front of the villa, the one-year sabbatical spent traveling in the Australian outback, the tasteful everyday wardrobe—as social beings we can read and classify the implicit messages of these "success stories". Perhaps people may set other priorities far away from the purchasable world of goods and services, but everyday reality proves that the mundane world of goods continues to move people and move them into action.

If one relates this ideological disposition of late modernity to collective forgiveness, then "living in the here and now" has a particular impact: It means that forgiveness is not transcended, that is, punishment and forgiveness (must) take place through supernatural instances, but must be decided and finally forgiven on the spot, that is, by the actors directly. Man is the forgiver. This is important because a world of hyper-connectedness cannot and will not afford to abort contact options, especially since the multiplicity of "right" and "wrong", of customs, conventions against the background of an innumerable number of contacts allows just as many possibilities of misinterpreted or dishonest behavior. Even ethics today disintegrates into many ethics—thus the freedom of the individual in Western countries is set without question, in Asian cultural areas, however, the primacy of the group over the individual continues to have an effect.

Despite all the scientific-analytical diagnoses of the deep currents of a theory of collective forgiveness, forgiveness remains a civilizational dinosaur in a world of laws, specifications, standardizations, regulations, ordinances, instructions, and rules. Forgiveness, in its impulse, is not subject to any scheme, dramaturgy, or condition. People forgive each other or they do not succeed in this approach—arguments do not help. Thus, it is an archaic, almost chaotic act of aesthetic judgment and feeling, which is not a one-off event but always a process. This "mysteriousness" is a consequence of individual autonomy that is grounded in the fundamental mystery of the human being. This conducive-constructive energy uses the individual's strength and will to trust to ensure the group's ability to function.

The more a sociality is characterized by an underlying feeling of the lack of supra-individual meaningfulness, the more the atomization of everyday life is rapidly progressing, and neither politics, philosophy nor religion is able to convey relevance due to a global culture of indifference and arbitrariness, unattainable hyper-ideals such as public opinion take over the function of orientation and give existence an at least imagined meaning.

Regardless, forgiveness is a profoundly human act. Forgiveness is an attempt to escape for moments the increasing loss of the individual, of one's own in the contemporary staccato of constant standardized change, and to decide autonomously and in parts argumentatively—feeling. Forgiveness contains the promise in a structured world of being "fully human"—wild, unpredictable, and free. To be and have meaning per se. As collective forgiveness, we vicariously participate and benefit from this uplifting sensation.

Hardly any contemporary work of art conveys the search for meaning, significance, and intuitive truths of late modernity more metaphorically impressively than Antony Gormley's sculptural installation "Another Place" (Fig. 7.1):

Fig. 7.1 Antony Gormley|Another Place, 1997 |Cast iron | 100 elements: each 189 × 53 × 29 cm | Installation view, Stavanger, Norway, 1998 |Photograph by Dag Mirestrand| © the artist

As individuals, we are always separated from each other and yet we seek proximity. Our gaze wanders in the same direction, it concerns the touching experiences of life that have always been important.

Let us not fool ourselves: To be human is to be able to be chaotic. To act against all logic. Only then does life come alive. Not as isolated loners, but to find the other as unique human beings. The dissolution of traditional forms of social bonds has not reduced the need for belonging to a community, for deep roots—on the contrary.

If there are still places that escape the "same" of hypermodernity, then it is the threatened reserves of friendship and love. Where purposes cease and forgiveness is possible.